British Columbia
TIME OF OUR LIVES

British Columbia

TIME OF OUR LIVES

Douglas & McIntyre
Vancouver/Toronto

Douglas & McIntyre Ltd.
1615 Venables Street
Vancouver, British Columbia V5L 2H1

Canadian Cataloguing in Publication Data

Main entry under title:

British Columbia, time of our lives

ISBN 0-88894-498-5

1. British Columbia — Description and travel — 1981-
Views. FC3817.4.B7 1986   917.11'0022'2   C86-091050-4
F1087.B7 1986

Photographs of British Columbia Pavilion (after half-title page)
and boats in a marina (after contents page) by Peter Timmermans.
Photograph of Spectrum Range (on frontispiece) by Gary Fiegehen.

Every effort has been made to identify and credit all sources used in
this book; any further information received will be acknowledged in
subsequent editions.

Commemorating British Columbia's role as Host Province of EXPO
86, this book has been published in co-operation with the B.C.
Pavilion Corporation, whose assistance and support is gratefully
acknowledged by the publisher.

The B.C. Pavilion is a Crown Corporation of the Province of British
Columbia.

The Honourable Patrick L. McGeer, Minister of International Trade
and Investment, and Minister Responsible for the B.C. Pavilion at
EXPO 86.

Design by Barbara Hodgson
Typesetting by PolaGraphics Ltd.
Colour separations by Cleland-Kent Western Ltd.
Printed in Canada by Agency Press
Bound in Canada by North-West Bindery Ltd.

CONTENTS

*British Columbia . . . if I had known what
it was like, I wouldn't have been content
with a mere visit. I'd have been born here.*
— Stephen Leacock

*T*hese words of Canada's most loved
humourist are typical of the fascina-
tion with which other Canadians, indeed
people of other nations, have long
viewed our special province.

FOREWORD

British Columbia is a favoured
land, rich in beauty as only a
province that stretches from the slopes of
the Canadian Rockies west to the shores of
the Pacific Ocean can be. With an abundance of timber, minerals, farmland, fish and
hydroelectric power, British Columbia's
wealth is present for all to see upon the
mountains and the northern prairies, on the
interior deserts and mist-shrouded coast.
Our greatest treasure, however, is the determined and resourceful people who are at
home in this land of natural glory.

Blessed as our province is with potential,
the challenge of reaping the benefits has
been immense. The scale of the land
overwhelms human activity. It takes
courage and determination to tackle the
challenge of huge distances and untamed
wilderness, towering mountains and
powerful rivers; to push roads and railways
through this rugged country; to build
mines, cut timber and plant crops.

We ask much of our land, from the
beauty and recreational opportunities it
offers to the resources that sustain the

A wonderful work of architecture, Lions
Gate Bridge soars over the waters of
Burrard Inlet and grandly marks the
entrance to Vancouver's harbour. Vancouver is Canada's third-largest city, and its
port is one of the busiest on the Pacific
coast of North America. *Peter Timmermans*

livelihood of our people and our place in the world economy. Developing those riches and bringing them to market has always been a challenge. And it has always been met.

British Columbia's growth and development would not have been possible without the energy of the men and women who live here. They succeeded in bettering themselves and their society through ingenuity, determination and hard work. That same spirit, together with an enthusiastic sense of adventure, is alive in our people today.

For British Columbians, this is a special time in our lives. We are now poised at the start of a new era. First, we learned how to harvest the gifts of land and water, as well as how to replenish where needed, to manage carefully, to preserve areas of wild beauty for the enjoyment of residents and

Determined drillers use their rig to bite deep into the province's abundant reserves of natural gas.
Peter Bennett

visitors. In the process of making the best use of our resources, we also developed new skills and technologies. Now the task is to find new markets for our products and expertise.

British Columbia has always looked outward to the world. From our early days we have sought out international markets, and we have long-standing ties of trade with many nations. Now is the time for us to start broadening our relationships with our trading partners around the world.

Our potential is truly exciting. This book celebrates that potential and the spirit of

At the busy Port of Vancouver, domestic and foreign freighters load containers and other cargo for delivery to overseas markets. *Peter Timmermans*

the people of British Columbia. In photographs and words, it portrays our achievements and indicates how we will fulfill our promise. Our people are miners and loggers, but also merchant bankers and champion athletes. Our people are skilled bridge-builders and masters of high technology, but also writers and artists. We are a diverse and gifted people whose lives are an extension of the land.

Through this special book, British Columbians can share a sense of our spectacular province with each other as well as with visitors. And as host of a world exposition, we are celebrating our pride in this place and its people through the British Columbia Pavilion on the Expo 86 site.

Our society is enriched by the contribution of those who came before us, the early settlers who had the enthusiasm and desire to stay and turn their opportunities into success. The accomplishments so evident today are an assurance that British Columbians will rise to the challenge of tomorrow. The current generation, building upon that solid foundation, is putting in place a legacy that will stand for years to come.

William R. Bennett, P.C.
Premier of the Province of
British Columbia

13

CHALLENGES

One of the world's largest aluminum smelting complexes, the Alcan Works in
Kitimat produces some 268 000 tonnes of aluminum ingots each year. *Lloyd Sutton*

CHALLENGES

Of British Columbia, Rudyard Kipling once wrote, "such a land is good for an energetic man."

Here was a land stretching east from the Pacific Ocean to the heights of the Rocky Mountains, north from the American border to the Yukon, with 27 000 kilometres of coastline cut into its rocky Pacific side and range after range of mountains running up its back like so many declarations of impassability. It would have required energy merely to contemplate it.

Think, then, about the energy required to do something about it, with it. There was obvious wealth, yes: salmon teeming in the rivers and sea, trees so ubiquitous that, early on, they were considered a real problem (they got in the way) and so big that, once felled, a single specimen could yield timber for several houses. A series of gold finds between 1850 and 1898 sent men rushing to the province's riverbeds and sent rushing after them all the men and women who provided services in the boom towns. The first farms were born to feed the hungry prospectors, and this has been the story in British Columbia: resource wealth provided the means by which a whole system of services, a whole network of towns and cities, could thrive.

Also arriving, from the start, were people of all sorts: Chinese and Japanese, European and English, and settlers from other Canadian provinces who would not stop until they reached salt water.

From the 1950s to the 1970s, British Columbia matured and developed. Huge hydroelectric projects generated needed power. Highways were cut into the Interior. This was also a golden period for British Columbia, when the world appetite for its resources seemed unbounded and so did

the store of those materials in the province's vault.

But the last world recession brought an enormous new challenge to the province. The challenge was to broaden its connections with the world market to offer not only resources but a whole range of new products and ideas.

British Columbia was also coming to understand the limits of its own resources. Tree-farming and fishing grounds management had long been practised, but suddenly they seemed not merely important but absolutely vital.

In its own history is the proof that B.C. can meet new challenges. The astonishing way in which men and women conquered and harnessed and found comfort within their wild, magnificent province in so few

years is demonstration of their potential. The challenges of today could hardly exceed those of the past. Today British Columbians are creating and applying new technologies to fish-farming, silviculture, sawmilling and mineral exploration, as well as developing a whole range of exciting new products. These technologies and products, invented in the course of harvesting the province's own resources, are themselves commodities in demand on world markets.

British Columbians can always look to their land for the essential definition of their prospects. They can be saved by its beauty, grandeur, wealth and variety, and by their own place — their own history and responsibilities and possibilities — in such a land.

From B.C.'s coastal forests to markets in Europe and Japan, some 1200 tonnes of prime, bleached pulp leave Westar Timber's Prince Rupert mill daily. *Gary Fiegehen*

Facing page. Working beneath the earth or deep in the forests or kilometres out on the seas, the men and women who harvest the province's primary resources do it with skill, pride and respect for the land. *Al Harvey*

Previous page. The mighty Columbia River, third longest in North America, is harnessed in B.C. by four hydroelectric dams, largest of which is the Revelstoke Dam. *Don McRae*

In today's modern surface mining operations, coal miners are actually heavy equipment operators who run the world's biggest vehicles. *Gary Fiegehen*

Facing page. Westar's Balmer surface coal mine in southeastern B.C. covers 1200 hectares of mountainous terrain. It straddles a rich coal belt that contains more than 225 million tonnes of clean coal, enough to supply present and future customers well into the twenty-first century. *Gary Fiegehen*

I've been in the mining industry forty-five years and no two decades have been the same. It's a continual challenge. I do like the people in mining, right from those digging it out to those in the financing. They all feel involved.

Walter Riva
Past Chairman of the Board,
BCRIC

Growing up in the Kootenays in the 1930s, I knew if you didn't work for a mining company, you didn't work. I first panned for gold when I was ten, and at university I took geology and chemistry. It's been the most exciting life in the world — you meet the doers and the shakers and the people with dreams.

Doug Elsdon
Geologist, assay consultant

A very positive thing over the twenty-three years of energy development in this province is that we have met the current demands of a steadily growing provincial economy as well as provided a surplus of clean power for the future. We have built an important energy base.

Ralph Spinney
Construction manager,
Revelstoke Hydroelectric
Project

*C*anadians are highly respected in the world of miners; we have developed a broad range of technical expertise.

Many foreign countries use us for our expertise developed here. We've worked in sixteen countries on the Pacific Rim alone.

Even today, the fellow who takes mining or metallurgy or geological engineering has to be an explorer. He has to be interested in what the layout is, what it looks like way out there on the edge of things. Yes, he has to be an explorer and a bit of an entrepreneur.

Harold Wright
Chairman, Wright Engineers
Ltd.

*N*atural gas is one of B.C.'s most abundant, low-cost energy resources, with broad distribution throughout the Interior and Lower Mainland. It is used by businesses, industries and hundreds of thousands of households. There is an exciting future for the natural gas industry here. Our plentiful supply creates the opportunity for additional exports and new domestic uses such as the growing utilization of natural gas as an automotive fuel.

R. E. (Bob) Kadlec
President and CEO, Inland
Natural Gas Co. Ltd.

Westshore Terminals' huge, 16-hectare coal-handling facility at Roberts Bank is the largest bulk terminal on the west coast of North America. From here, coal mined in B.C.'s Interior goes to markets in the Pacific Rim, Europe and Latin America — 20 million tonnes a year. *Gary Fiegehen*

Facing page. Gigantic packhorses, these 180-tonne-capacity trucks are loaded with coal for transport to unit-trains that head for the Roberts Bank port. About 900 litres of antifreeze per truck are needed to keep the massive vehicles moving through severe winter conditions. *Gary Fiegehen*

Next page. Once considered a useless by-product of the gas-refining process, sulphur is now used extensively in the manufacture of pulp and fertilizer. Huge piles of the bright yellow mineral await shipment to national and international markets. *Lloyd Sutton*

GAS & OIL: THE NEW GOLD

*F*ar beneath the plains and foothills of northeastern British Columbia lie rich reserves of the province's largest revenue producer — natural gas. Over 600 gas and 700 oil wells in this area provide fuel for homes and industries throughout the province, as well as for the export market. The production value of B.C.'s oil and gas industry is about one billion dollars a year.

Natural gas, a major export commodity, is distributed to customers in the province and the United States via more than 12 000 kilometres of pipeline. That is enough pipe

1 In the remote northeast corner of British Columbia, the gas and oil harvested today began its formation more than a hundred million years ago.
2 To search for gas and oil in inaccessible areas, helicopters drop off crews as well as boxes filled with electronic equipment and computers.
3 *and* 4 Canada's first wells were drilled with a "pole-tool" rig — a bit on the end of a black ash pole, which was dropped from a wooden derrick. Today's rigs rely on engines instead of gravity to push down towards the gas or oil below.

5 An orderly mass of pipes, this refinery near Fort St. John is two plants in one and processes both gas and oil piped to it from nearby wells.

6 Two hundred people work at this gas and oil refinery on the bank of the Peace River, producing 15.5 million cubic metres of gas and 20 500 barrels of oil a day.

7 Flares like this are the gas industry's most dramatic symbol. They regulate pipeline pressure, acting as a kind of safety valve by burning off excess product.

Photographs by Peter Bennett

Not only is natural gas an abundant source of energy, it is one of the cheapest and most versatile. For sale to overseas markets, gas is liquefied so that it can be shipped by tanker, then reconverted to its original state for use. Gas can also be compressed for use as an alternative auto fuel to gasoline.

At gas processing plants, valuable by-products are removed, including propane, which is used for heating, and methanol, which is used as a gasoline additive. Sulphur, an impurity removed from gas, is used as a component of fertilizer.

Yet for all the technology used to refine gas and oil and get them to market, as well as in geographic, seismic and geological studies to discover new reserves, the gas and oil industry continues to exist on a very human scale. There is a saying in the oil patch that "oil is found in the minds of men." And most often it is people whose intuition leads to just the right place to drill a producing well.

With huge assured supplies of energy that include hydroelectricity, coal and oil as well as natural gas, the province's industries can make long-term plans with confidence.

Previous page. Throughout this century, the forest industry has depended on skilled loggers to feed its sawmills and pulp mills. *Robert Semeniuk*

A triumphant logger rests after falling a huge tree. In 1912 North America's tallest tree, 125 metres in height, was felled in North Vancouver. It alone yielded over 100 000 board feet of lumber, enough to build nine modern houses. *Al Harvey*

With much of B.C.'s lumber processed in local mills, the rivers are highways for massive log booms. The workers who handle the booms are highly skilled, timing with precision the movements of logs and river. *Chuck O'Rear, Image Finders*

*A*re we still perceived as hewers of wood? Well, when half the economy is about hewing wood, I guess we'd have to be. Anyway, we're damn good hewers of wood. There has been lots of talk about forestry as a sunset industry. Well, that's absolutely not true. The development of high-tech procedures is complementary to our traditional operations.

Ray Smith
President and Chief Executive Officer, MacMillan Bloedel Ltd.

*O*ne example of progress is the co-operation developing between formerly antago- nistic camps. Now we've reached the point where foresters are regarding the environment from the stand- point of recreational oppor- tunities and habitat consider- ations — they are no longer looking at trees as two-by- fours with needles.

Graham Kenyon
Head of environmental control, Cominco (Trail, B.C.), and conservationist

33

*T*here's an enormous potential in technology to improve the cost-efficiency of fire-detection. The technique of line-mapping is not new, but we've started using it in new ways, especially for sorting out how to get to lightning-caused fires and to map fire perimeters and hot spots. We also use LANDSAT satellite imagery to assess fire perimeters after the fire is finished. With air patrols, lookouts and ground patrols, the whole range of our fire-detection work alone costs about $2 million a year. We also do a lot in the whole area of fire prevention.

In addition to our large firefighting program, we have a specially trained unit of thirty crew members called Rapattack. They fight about 150 fires a summer. This program and its management structure was difficult to implement. It has been duplicated by other agencies and the Americans are interested in reviewing it.

We have a real edge in terms of our air operations. We have some medium helicopters with bombing tanks, and our air tanker fleet is one of the biggest in the world.

Dave Gilbert (Manager, Planning Development and Research Protection Branch), Jim Dunlop (Co-ordinator, Fire Preparedness Protection Branch), Ministry of Forests

Summer brings the forests to tinder dryness, and forest fires destroy one of the province's most valuable resources. Each spring, seedlings are planted to repair the damage nature has done. *Government of British Columbia*

Facing page. Sometimes fires are deliberately set to rid logged areas of debris. Slash burning is carefully controlled, and ash from the fire helps the growth of trees planted soon after. *R.A. Farquhar, Image Finders*

Previous page. Years ago, sawmills regarded wood chips as a waste product. Today, the B.C. pulp and paper industry purchases those wood chips, a great sea of them like this scene in Crofton, and from this former waste produces 5 million tonnes of pulp a year. *Al Harvey*

RESOURCES: HELPING NATURE

1 governments will also spend some $300 million and replant some 150 000 hectares with juvenile trees.

Dramatic changes have also occurred in the management of the province's fish resources. The federal-provincial salmonid enhancement program adds close to 23 million kilograms of salmon annually. The province also operates an extensive hatchery program for fresh-water fish. While separate from the resource management programs, the aquaculture industry has the potential to enormously increase the province's total fish resources.

Mineral resources are now mined so that the land can be reclaimed for other uses, and controls are in place to maintain the ecological balance and reduce pollution.

The natural bounty that has always been a part of British Columbia's heritage is today nurtured, managed and protected to ensure that the province's resources will flourish in the years to come.

1 The forests of the future are carefully tended. These juvenile douglas-firs will eventually be planted in new forests, and will have every chance of growth that research and technology can offer.
2 To maintain the forest inventory, logged and burned areas are replanted with 100 million trees each year. The seedlings are raised in a dozen enormous nurseries in the province.
3 Aquaculture's newest crop is kelp. The plants are often cultivated in nets suspended from rafts for easy checking and protection from predators.
4 When young salmon run down the rivers in which they hatched to live in the sea, it will be years before they return to spawn and die. Biologists tag the salmon to keep track of their populations and to monitor migration routes.

Photographs by Doug Wilson, Image Finders (1); Image Finders (2); Image West (3); Chuck O'Rear, Image Finders (4)

*F*or decades, the early settlers in British Columbia, awed by the abundance of natural resources, took freely from the forests, hills, oceans and streams. With population growth, technological advances and expanding markets, the seemingly infinite supply of fish and forest was abruptly recognized to be finite.

To ensure an ongoing supply of trees and to protect the multibillion-dollar forest industry, the B.C. government has introduced a silviculture program that includes pest-control measures. Within the five-year span of the program, provincial and federal

3

4

Their catch unloaded, fishing boats rock
at berth in Nanaimo harbour. Tomorrow,
their buoys will again mark the location of
their nets as they fish for Pacific salmon.
Peter Bennett

Facing page. Nets hang to dry along the
waterfront in the Lower Mainland fishing
community of Steveston.
Ken Straiton, Image Finders

Next page. Fishing boats lie at anchor
along the Steveston waterfront. While the
number of fishermen has dropped in
recent years, technical advances have
increased efficiency. *James O'Mara*

*I*t's a gold-rush mentality to
get involved with aqua-
culture. It's just crazy. The
highest visibility is with fin
fish, but really it's right across
the board. It is especially important that we work to get
some systems in place for the
good of the whole aqua-
culture industry. Things like
disease monitoring, and general product, quality technical things. We have to guard
against a boom-and-bust
situation.

With any luck — and I
mean luck entailing the
support of governments in
establishing an infrastructure
— and with the industry
organized on a realistic basis,
we are going to be bigger than
the fisheries before the year
2000.

In our own operation we've
gone from two families to
seventy-three employees in
six months.

David Saxby
Chairman, Pacific Aqua Foods

Skilled workers quickly process a day's catch for canning. Huge quantities of salmon leave B.C. canneries annually to reappear on dinner tables around the world. *Image West Photography*

Facing page. Seiners, the largest boats of B.C.'s salmon fishing fleet, loop huge nets into the ocean, then gather in their silvery catch. *Don McRae*

Next page. Agriculture is the province's fourth largest industry, and from its fields come meat and dairy products, as well as rich harvests of grain, fruits and vegetables that are enjoyed by consumers here and abroad. *Pat Morrow, Image Finders*

*O*ne thing to be hopeful about is the next phase of the salmonid enhancement program. To be successful it's going to require further investment above sustaining levels, probably as much as $200 million over five years. But certainly the results of the first five-year phase are quite good.

We've also come a long way in the area of general environmental issues. Although there are continuing conflicts between resource users (forestry versus fisheries, for example), there is significant progress.

The way the fishery is being managed now also gives me some basis for optimism. In the five years 1980–84 the catch averaged 65 000 tonnes, substantially lower than in the previous five-year period. In 1985 though, the catch was 100 000 tonnes. Our aim should really be to level out at about 85 000 tonnes per year.

We export between 65 and 70 per cent of our production each year. In the past that has been about $360 million dollars a year. Japan and the European Economic Community buy our frozen salmon, and the U.K. and Australia buy our canned salmon.

Mike Hunter
President, Fisheries Council
of British Columbia

I ranch near Princeton. My grandfather was one of the first white settlers in the upper end of the Similkameen valley. There have been a lot of changes here. But you're bound to have change if there's progress.

There has been a real trend for people to move out of the urban areas into the countryside, on a fairly large scale. This causes a lot of management problems in the cattle business. You can't range cattle through people's back yards.

A very positive change has been rural electrification. This has taken place on a large scale and more than anything else has done an awful lot to improve the capabilities of rural agricultural land. It enabled ranchers especially to get into irrigation schemes to significantly improve the productivity of their land.

Harold Allison
President, B.C. Federation
of Agriculture

Cattle ranches in the B.C. Interior send tonnes of beef to market yearly. Although the snowmobile, truck and trail bike are now standard equipment, at roundup time the cowboy and his horse are still a familiar sight. *Al Harvey*

Facing page, top. In the shadow of the hills where cattle have grazed since gold-rush days, livestock today forage only as far as the feeding pen. *Derek and Jane Abson, Photo/Graphics*

Facing page, bottom. Hands hardened from decades of holding ropes and reins, and face creased from the sun and wind, the working cowboy bears little resemblance to his urban imitators. *Image West Photography*

There are about three thousand acres of vines in B.C. The overall acreage is quite stable.

The wine business is undergoing an interesting transformation in B.C. There has been an evolution in our wines — our wine quality has never been better. Our consumers will attest to this. The major commercial wineries are producing selected fine wines, better wines than they've ever produced. As well, the estate winery business has blossomed. These high-priced, high-quality wines really help to promote the image of our products. They are the best wines in Canada.

We have fifty years' experience in making wine here. The Europeans have hundreds. It takes some time to establish the right wines, the right processes. As our industry matures, we can only get better.

Lee Sienna
Vice-President, Casabello
Wines, and President, B.C.
Wine Council

In the dim seclusion of the vat room in one of B.C.'s many wineries, a welder works while the year's vintage ages around him. Over a dozen B.C. vintners bottle a variety of wines each year. *Gary Fiegehen*

Irrigation has turned the sunny semidesert
of the southern Interior valleys into lush
orchards and vineyards suited for the
growth of tree fruits and grapes.
Gary Fiegehen

A major construction project, the 465-metre Annacis Island bridge is the longest cable-stayed bridge in the world. It provides access to the island's industrial park, as well as a route for commuters to get from suburbs to Vancouver. Bridges are vital for Vancouver, which is built on a river delta. *Stirling Ward Photographic Design*

Facing page, top and bottom. Vancouver more and more reflects an international influence, as people, investments and businesses arrive to add flair and dimension to this city of over one million people. Construction in the downtown core creates an ever-changing skyline for Canada's third largest city.
Michelle Normoyle

*T*he B.C. construction industry has had to work in enormously varied conditions geographically. We have built a lot of pulp mills and a lot of mines. There is no doubt that we have gained a real expertise in engineering and construction matters.

A number of firms in British Columbia do work overseas, and Vancouver, especially on the engineering side, does quite a bit in pulp and paper and mining. Overseas projects take hundreds of supervisors and tradesmen.

R. J. Meyers
President, Dominion
Construction

CONNECTIONS

Squat, powerful tugboats, dwarfed by the barges they pull, connect coastal ports and help move the province's resources out to world markets. *Gary Fiegehen*

CONNECTIONS

The ability to move materials and words determines the nature of any society, and transportation and communication have presented special challenges in British Columbia. The problem was simply that British Columbians usually wanted to move huge and heavy things — like trees and ore — over terrain whose very beauty was a measure also of its difficulty. And from the first gold rush in the nineteenth century to the rush of a northern coal train this morning, they have been in a hurry to do it.

Advanced technology was the lure that brought British Columbia into Confederation in 1871 — the promise by Canada's first Prime Minister of a transcontinental railway to link the colony to the rest of the nation. The west coast British colony then lacked even an east-west wagon road over the mountains. Moving north-south, up the valleys, was hard enough, and construction of the Ladner-Barkerville wagon road to the Cariboo region and its gold had been a tremendous feat. When the last spike of the transcontinental railway was driven in 1885, a single transportation and communication line assured the place of British Columbia in the young country. The opportunities for the province seemed unlimited. By 1910 B.C. had 6000 kilometres of railway, and counting. As trails turned into roads and railways, towns appeared — some to die when companies moved or dissolved, others to remain and grow as important regional centres. Anyone who knows the province cannot look at a road map without wondering at the determination needed to push those roads to where they eventually went. And the work goes on: half a billion dollars were spent in three years to drive a B.C. Rail line to the northeast coal site by 1983. In the south, the first stretch of the new Coquihalla Highway was

nearing completion at the end of 1985, a spectacular accomplishment.

From the beginning, new ways of transporting and communicating were eagerly embraced. As early as 1877 a British Columbian was experimenting with telephone technology, and by 1886 a telegraph line had crossed the country. The first automobile arrived in 1901. The first Canadian-built airplane was flown in B.C. in 1910, by a man who later crashed it into a Victoria cow pasture (he survived), and the first woman in Canada to fly an airplane did so on Lulu Island in 1913.

How would the British Columbia of today appear to those pioneers? They would surely be pleased by the way things and words move about (and over) the still-difficult terrain. They would find a web of highways connecting communities; railway

lines carrying gargantuan shipments of coal and cars and wheat to and from some of the busiest ports on the Pacific; a fleet of ferries running from the mainland to Vancouver Island, through the Inland Passage and up the coast; airplanes flying where no roads can go, and a telecommunications system that not only links the once-isolated province to Canada and to the rest of the world but has stitched the province closer together at the same time.

In British Columbia, products and ideas will change, and the means of moving them, but this is a province that always has and always will understand the critical importance of good connections.

Satellite dishes made by B.C.'s Microtel Pacific Research sit and receive telephone and computer signals that bring people around the world closer together. *Gary Fiegehen*

Facing page. The sailors and ships that move British Columbia's exports to overseas markets link the province to the world. *Dolores Baswick*

Previous page. As the sun crystallizes the waters of the Strait of Georgia, seafaring nuns enjoy the beauty of the Gulf Islands from the deck of B.C. Ferry's *Queen of Saanich*. *P. Andras Dancs, North Light Images*

Riding on a cushion of air above the waves, the Canadian Coast Guard hovercraft provides rescue along British Columbia's long coastline. *Gordon Lafleur*

One thing that we do very, very well at present is move people around across a lot of water. We developed a first-class ferry system that runs up and down the coast as well as amongst the coastal islands, and from Vancouver Island to the mainland. We have also developed a vessel traffic management system so sophisticated that people come from other parts of the world to look at it.

We build some of the finest highways in the world, but there are many parts of this province where the terrain is just too difficult — where it's just too expensive to cut roads or run in rail lines. And here is where satellite remote sensing comes in. It can be used to identify the optimum routes for access to places. It bodes well for us that it is here in British Columbia that so much of this extremely sophisticated technology is being developed.

And where the places are too remote, or too expensive to reach for other reasons — well, I'm confident that airships are going to be used to get those minerals or that timber out. B.C has a history of innovation in this area — getting bulk resources out to market.

Leslie Millin
Director, The 1986 World
Exposition Symposium Series

*I*n every maritime city, the heart of that city is its port. From here the city grows out, rail lines and roads begin and end, cargoes from the far corners of the globe arrive, and shipments for distant ports leave. It is the place from which the adventuring seaman leaves, the home to which the weary sailor returns. The Port of Vancouver, the busiest port on the Pacific Coast of the Americas, is also one of the most beautiful. Ringed by mountains, the harbour sits tranquil and placid, oblivious to the storms that may rage outside its shelter.

Each year some 2300 ships flying the flags of more than fifty nations slip under Lions Gate Bridge to dock in the harbour. These include the elegant cruise ships that

1 Viewed from the top of one of Vanterm's giant container cranes, ocean-going liners look like toy ships in the harbour.
2 Straddle carriers hoist a container from its flatbed truck one step closer to its eventual loading into a ship's hold.
3 Vanterm's big site is largely given over to a storage area for containers. Here, the boxes wearing names of shippers from around the globe await the move to their next destination.

4 Row upon row of neatly
stacked piles of lumber await
shipment to markets in Asia
and Europe.
5 Seaboard Shipping's hulking
Ro/Ro vessels carry enough
lumber at one time to build all
the houses in a small
community.
6 Outward bound, the *Malahat*
is one of many vessels on
which lumber from B.C. mills
goes to build houses in
distant parts of the world.

4 each year bring more than 160 000 travellers to highlight their holidays with a stop
in Vancouver.

The first shipment from the harbour was
a small load of lumber, which sailed from
a mill on its north side for the nearby town
of New Westminster. Today, while lumber
shipments are still a significant part of the
cargo carried, ships also head out with coal,
grain, petroleum products and chemicals.
Since the advent of containerized shipping,
massive container ships now make up a
sizable proportion of the vessels loading at
Port of Vancouver docks.

Containerization created a need for
highly specialized and technologically
advanced equipment. The Vanterm container facility, located on a 31-hectare site,
is one of the most sophisticated of such
facilities in North America. Here, giant
high-speed cranes dwarf the largest of the
ships they service as they load and unload
the containers.

Equally impressive is the Seaboard
International Terminal, a massive,
lumber-exporting complex that bears
little resemblance to the primitive, early
lumber-shipping facilities. From here,
the unique Ro/Ro's sail. These specially
designed lumber vessels (Ro/Ro is the
abbreviation for "roll-on/roll-off," the
means by which lumber is loaded and
unloaded) carry 18 to 20 million board feet
of lumber at a time, enough to build about
2000 three-bedroom houses.

While the mammoth freighters and cruise
ships move in and out of the harbour, the
tiny kayaks, rowing skiffs, and sailboats are
a constant reminder that the Port of Vancouver, like ports around the globe, does
not handle goods for destinations, it
handles goods for people.

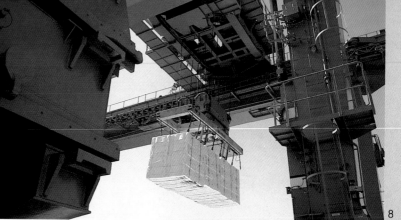

7 To the drydocks at Burrard Yarrows in Vancouver Harbour come ships from some fifty shipping lines for repairs. As well, new ships are built and launched here.

8 Huge steel arms have replaced human strength to move goods in port. Now, mechanical towers as tall as office buildings load and unload container ships.

9 From small pleasure craft to giant freighters to ferries plying the Strait of Georgia, all are monitored through the sophisticated electronic tracking and guidance systems of Vancouver's Harbour Traffic Control.

10 In the quiet hum of night, lights on ships at berth illuminate the loading of another hold. While other industries can pause for sleep, the harbour is never silent.

Photographs by Peter Timmermans (1–3); Jürgen Vogt, Photo/Graphics (4, 10); Dolores Baswick (5, 6); Randy Bradley (7); Gary Fiegehen (8); Martin Roland (9)

Top. Four years and one billion dollars in the making, the new rapid-transit SkyTrain runs 22 kilometres from New Westminster to the harbour in downtown Vancouver.
Colin Jewall, B.C. Transit

Bottom. Each year, more than twelve million residents and visitors, along with trucks, buses and cars sail the waters of the Strait of Georgia aboard ferry boats. Serving island cities like Victoria and Nanaimo, the B.C. Ferry Corporation's government-owned fleet is one of the largest such operations in the world.
Thomas Bruckbauer

Facing page. Streamlined and efficient, the SeaBus provides a unique water link across Vancouver Harbour for commuters.
Lloyd Sutton

Western Canada has had to establish very efficient transportation services to carry its exports over the long distances they need to cover to get to market.

Bulk transport is an area in which B.C. has had to excel. The surmounting of enormous physical barriers, the development of systems to move huge quantities of material in bulk — this has given us significant expertise.

The challenge for the future is the same as the challenge in the past. We must continue to search for more efficient ways of moving our goods to market.

Professor Trevor D. Heaver
Director, Centre for
Transportation Studies

Our towboat technology is leading edge. It involves, for example, a system of towboats and barges — more than a thousand vessels — moving logs, chips, pulp and paper products, cement, gravel and oil. There is a water highway up and down the coast, and the tonnage handled is of the order of 60 million metric tonnes per year — more than the entire St. Lawrence Seaway.

Martin Crilly
President, Western
Transportation Advisory
Council

Powerful B.C. Rail locomotives pull trains loaded with forestry products, coal, sulphur and grain to tidewater for shipment to markets. A passenger service acts as a vital link to homes and towns from North Vancouver to Prince George.
Gary Fiegehen.

Facing page. Up-ended by a giant hydraulic lift as though it were a toy, a container truck offloads at the Vancouver docks. *Gary Fiegehen*

Previous page. From these cables hang the 470-metre span of the Lions Gate Bridge, an exhilarating half-crescent in the sky. For nearly half a century the famous landmark has linked Vancouver's North Shore to the downtown core.
Robert Semeniuk

COQUIHALLA: MOUNTAIN HIGHWAY

1

*N*ine million tonnes of gravel. Forty-five kilometres of culvert pipe. Six hundred and twenty-five dump-truck loads of gravel. Seven hundred thousand seraper loads of dirt. A hundred and sixty thousand tonnes of concrete. Twenty-six thousand four hundred tonnes of steel. Eight hundred thousand cubic metres of stripping. Ninety thousand metres of fencing. A hundred and fifty thousand metres of median and guard rail . . . and that is just the first of three phases.

Using so many men and so much material and equipment that even these actual statistics fade beneath the sheer enormity of the project, the largest road-building undertaking in North America is underway. The Coquihalla Highway is not just pushing four lanes of superhighway for 115 kilometres at a cost of a quarter of a billion dollars, but doing it in half the time it would normally take with the help of 26 000 direct and indirect workers.

The Coquihalla Highway, the largest and most ambitious highway project in

1 Great Bear Snowshed, the world's longest at 185 metres as well as being six lanes in width, will keep avalanches from tumbling onto the highway.
2 Dry Gulch Bridge spans a deep gorge by stretching over it a 265-metre-long structural steel arch. Of the thirty-five bridges constructed in Phase I, it is the largest.
3 Loading up with a minute portion of the 9 million tonnes of gravel that form the bed for the asphalt, a truck makes another stop at the Coldwater gravel pit.
4 Fortunately, the weather was kind to the builders of the Coquihalla Highway. Anticipated snowfall levels were not reached, enabling builders to work through the normally inactive winter season.

5

6

7

5, 6, 7 and 8 With more than 750 pieces of heavy equipment on the job, the Coquihalla had the distinction of having the largest single concentration of such equipment in North America.

9 One of twelve earth-filled retaining walls along the highway takes form. To protect the sensitive salmon-spawning areas in rivers along the highway, only clean rock fill could be used near waterways.

Photographs by Ed Gifford

the province's history, involves more than laying a strip of asphalt from Hope to Merritt — and eventually on to Kamloops and then to Peachland in the Okanagan. It also involves constructing six diversion dams, four stopping dams, the world's largest snowshed and thirty-seven bridges in the first phase alone — all while protecting salmon-spawning grounds in the rivers and cattle ranges on the open plains.

Traffic on the Coquihalla Highway in summer is estimated at 10 000 vehicles per day. Once Phase II is completed and the road reaches Kamloops, the Coquihalla will be 80 kilometres shorter than the Fraser Canyon route on the Trans-Canada Highway and will save an hour of driving time. Travellers using the Phase I Merritt-to-Hope route will pay a toll to use the road. And as they skim through the scenic Coquihalla River valley and Boston Bar Creek valley at 100 kilometres per hour on British Columbia's newest and finest highway, they will be enjoying the result of the province's greatest road-building challenge.

The *New Republic* is one of the oldest Chinese-language newspapers in Canada and has been keeping readers informed since 1910. Vancouver's Chinatown, the largest in Canada, is a strong, proud and vital community. *Albert Chin*

It seems to me that if you really care about a story — about the news — you play straight with your readers. The community press is still pretty straight in this regard. And maybe it does have a sort of gosh-golly innocence. But it has become a significant force. I think this will continue.

Stanley Burke
Journalist

To be philosophical about it, the premise of a democratic and free society rests on the assumption of a broadly informed citizenry. I'm very committed to the whole concept of lifelong education. I believe that telecommunication technology will profoundly affect our ability to make achievable the notion of lifelong learning. We're using television to permit access to education to people otherwise isolated in the same way that putting through a new highway or some other transportation technology creates access in terms of people's mobility.

Dr. Glen M. Farrell
President, Knowledge Network

With the rapid passing of pieces of paper across the floor, traders measure the pulse of the province's economy. The Vancouver Stock Exchange is a barometer for Western Canadian resource industries.
Creative House

Even in this era of technological communication, when words can be transmitted across continents more rapidly than the human voice can speak them, the link between businesses is often forged by bicycle messengers racing through busy downtown streets. *Naomi Stevens*

*W*hen foreign partners or investment interests look at B.C., they see a very stable arena in which to do business. We should recognize this for the important asset it is. This is the beginning of what could be a golden era of Pacific Rim trade.

Arthur Hara
Chairman, Mitsubishi Canada Ltd., and Chairman, Vancouver Board of Trade

*V*ancouver's financial community is a creature of its own, a creature that still lives in part in the wild and woolly west. There are those raw, rugged characters, those flamboyant entrepreneurs, those boiler-room promoters. But perhaps that's the nature of a speculative market. After all, the Vancouver Stock Exchange prides itself as the junior venture capital exchange of the world.

Der Hoi-Yin
CBC National Television News

*B*ritish Columbia was discovered by traders — traders coming at it from the east overland and by sea along the coast. As a society, we were born, bred, and reared by traders. And as a result, we're pretty good at it.

The Honourable Don Phillips
Past Minister of International Trade and Investment

INNOVATIONS

At the TRIUMF research institution at the University of British Columbia, innovations like the particle accelerator have put its scientists at the leading edge of research in high-energy physics. *Peter Bennett*

INNOVATIONS

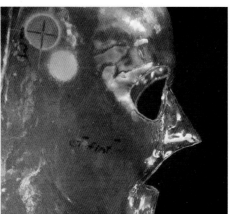

*P*oised on the western edge of the North American continent, in close touch with Europe and Asia through Canada's advanced telecommunications system (parts of which rely on British Columbian technology), B.C. is well placed to apply its resource wealth and technological expertise to the challenges of a new age. Experts say that the high-tech community in the province will soon reach "critical mass," a self-sustaining condition in which the number of companies, scientists, businessmen and ideas is such that they can feed off each other and rapidly expand.

Already, the electronics industry generates more money than the fisheries. Well-established companies are successfully marketing products in such diverse areas as microelectronic circuitry, satellite sensing technology, cellular telephone systems, computer software and deep-sea submersibles. The province also has a surprising and growing number of fledgling high-technology businesses, which are developing "muscles" for robots, genetically tinkering with plants and bacteria, and building laser-beam tape recorders; the range of their work is huge.

But British Columbia's natural resources are still its most important asset, and the province faces competition in every market. New technology can help in two ways: by establishing a competitive edge in a resource industry, and then by exporting the developed technology itself.

In forestry, B.C. companies are manufacturing new pest controls — based on chemical "ambrosias" — to lure beetles away from trees; they are cloning important timber species to develop a race of super trees, and they are manufacturing computer-controlled saws to reduce the amount of sawdust waste.

Dressed in a white sterile suit in an environment-controlled Clean Room, an engineer examines a custom-designed circuit wafer for complex electronic equipment. *Gary Fiegehen*

Facing page. One medical use of the particle accelerator at TRIUMF is to destroy cancer tumours in the brain, with the help of an immobilization mask. *Peter Bennett*

Previous page. Bringing high-tech people and ideas together, Discovery Park, at the B.C. Institute of Technology in Vancouver, is one of several government-funded research facilities in the province. *Jacques André*

Genetic engineering is also being applied to fish-farming, a business that may eventually overtake conventional fishing in importance. In mining, biological and other techniques are being applied to mineral extraction.

The universities are essential to the whole process. They provide a pool of resident expertise, educate students for the high-technology community and do pure scientific research. The TRIUMF cyclotron at the University of B.C., for example, which generates a high-intensity proton beam, is one of only three such facilities in existence. Several hundred scientists work there, applying the data it provides not only to theoretical experiments but also to medical, industrial and commercial use.

Recognizing that the interplay of ideas between businesses and schools is important, the provincial government set up the Discovery Foundation in the late 1970s to attract high-tech companies to B.C.

Discovery Parks, built next door to each of the three universities in the province, now hum with many of the province's most important research and development companies. In addition, the foundation operates an "incubator facility" at the B.C. Institute of Technology to pull promising businesses out of garages and basements. A Chinese government official, touring the three-year-old incubator building, enthusiastically described the mood as "mother hen with her baby chicks."

British Columbians are so familiar with the overwhelming physical presence of the land, so accustomed to the image of the logger and fisherman, to the wild expanses between populated areas in their province, that they are not necessarily aware of the scientists and tinkerers in their midst. But high technology is not a myth, not a dream. It is a constantly renewable resource, a rich field already being explored and promising bigger things for the future.

Locked in a clear acrylic sphere beneath the ocean, the pilot of Can-Dive's unique Deep Rover submersible has two sophisticated manipulator arms that allow tasks to be performed with the aid of tactile feedback. *Lou Lehmann*

Top. As at home in the water as the sea mammal whose name it bears, the Sea Otter was designed in North Vancouver for use as a submersible workstation in the oceans and lakes of the world.
Lou Lehmann

Bottom. Developed to replace the bulky, awkward underwater diving suits now in use, Can-Dive's Newtsuit is lightweight and good to depths of 225 metres.
Mark Atherton

Vancouver is a world-class technological centre for underwater work. The early work done here on the Pisces and other manned submersibles developed in the early 1960s has put Vancouver in the forefront of submarine technology, and it's a very prestigious position. For me, underwater is absolutely fascinating; sailing over a coral reef is like flying over a mountain range.

Dennis Hurd
President, Sub Aquatics
Development Corp.

HIGH TECH: SCIENCE & INGENUITY

*T*wenty years ago, when astronaut Neil Armstrong climbed down the ladder from his landing craft and, extending the first human foot onto the lunar surface, uttered the famous words: "A small step for man; a giant leap for mankind," it seemed to many that the culmination of the technological revolution had been reached. In fact, it was still in its infancy.

While the intricacies of high technology today are light years beyond the grasp of the average person, the results of its developments are felt — and enjoyed — by them daily.

Many B.C. companies and research groups have earned global acclaim for innovations that have probed and changed the world around us. At the forefront of this new high-tech industry are B.C. companies such as MacDonald Dettwiler and Associates, which develops products and systems using digital imaging to serve a wide range of applications. The information transmitted from satellites is translated into computer-generated pictures that can be used to forecast weather; discover oil and mineral deposits; map and track changes in the forests, oceans and atmosphere of the world, as well as monitor pollution control, ice movement in the Canadian Arctic and

1 The province's Lower Mainland as pictured by Landsat, an earth resource satellite, from 700 kilometres above the earth. MDA is the world leader in the production of ground stations to interpret this satellite's data.

2, 3 *and* 4 Special satellites supply data from which to forecast the weather with some degree of accuracy. Satellite images allow meteorologists to (2) identify weather systems, (3) track cyclone formations, and (4) monitor global cloud distributions with the ease of looking at a photograph.

2

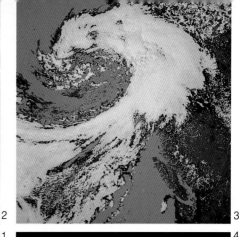

3

1

4

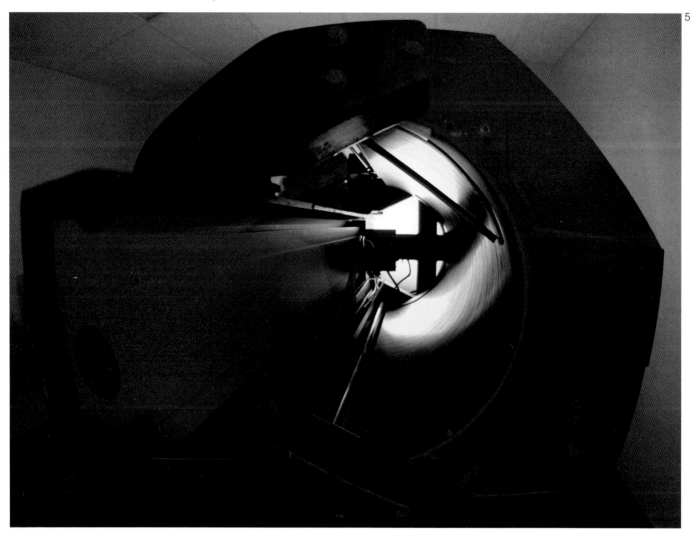

activities along borders and coastal waters.

Image-analysis systems developed by MDA can take satellite data and process it to display such information as land features, resource concentrations, temperature variations and changes in land use. This information can be printed or displayed with the same clarity and ease of interpretation as a road map or snapshot. From a satellite hundreds of kilometres above the earth, it is now possible, for example, to monitor the growth of crops in specific locations in the province.

5 MacDonald Dettwiler's laser photo-plotter, the FIRE 9000, is a technological innovation to make master plans for the production of printed circuit boards. This technology is the fastest and most accurate of its kind in the world today.

6 *and* 7 Landsat images can provide information on ground resources when coded to various colours for each mineral.

Photographs by MacDonald Dettwiler and Associates (1–4, 6, 7); Robert Semeniuk (5)

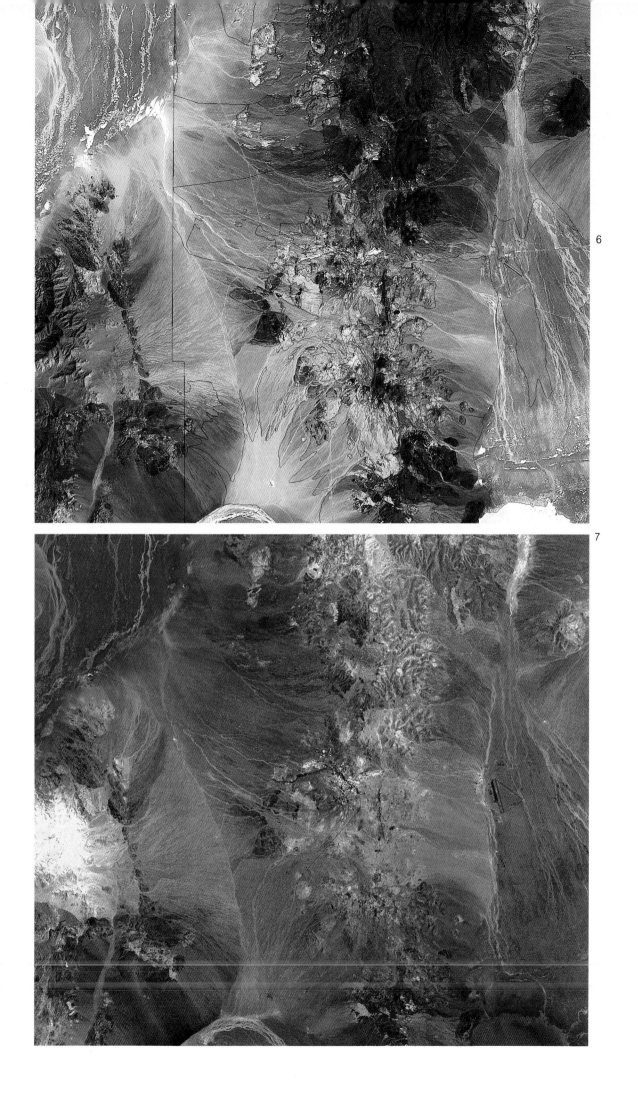

6

7

The only place we have the edge is in our know-how. Our competitive advantage lies in our educational system. The raw material of a knowledge-based industry is highly trained people — like trees to a forester or fish to a fisherman.

Dr. John MacDonald
Chairman of the Board,
MacDonald Dettwiler &
Associates Ltd.

The concept of antibiotics from plants is an ancient one. There are many cultures that use plant material to cure wounds and so forth. Some of these are very, very efficacious.

We have reason to think that there are many valuable chemicals in plants. Suddenly, a lot of people are interested.

We've become especially interested in these characteristics in the plants of British Columbia. There is a roadside weed that grows near Princeton and a few places in the Interior that contains really a very, very good antibiotic.

We didn't come across it by accident, though. We have been looking at this particular group of chemicals for about ten years.

Professor Neil Towers
Department of Botany,
University of British Columbia

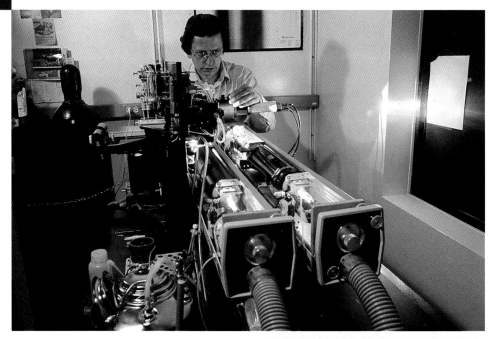

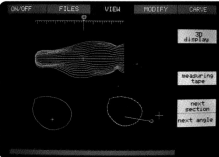

Top and bottom. Until now, the fitting of prostheses for below-the-knee amputations was a lengthy, uncomfortable process for the amputee. Now, in a major breakthrough, the Biomedical Engineering Resources Unit at the University of British Columbia has developed a computerized design system (bottom) to graph the contours of the amputee's stump. Having graphed the contours of the leg, the computer then controls a milling machine (top) to carve out a mold.
Dale Leniuk

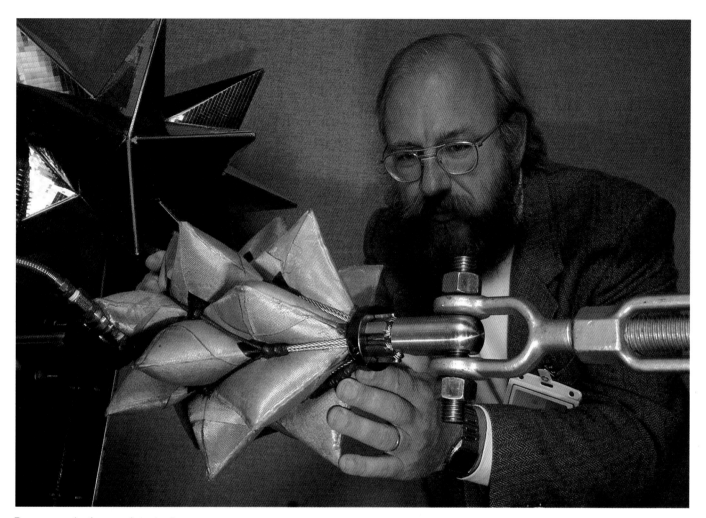

Romac, a robotic muscle actuator, was developed by MacDonald Dettwiler to produce a mechanical equivalent of human muscles. Such mechanical muscles have ten times more force than comparable pneumatic cylinders or electric motors. *Robert Semeniuk*

At B.C. Hydro's System Control Centre in Burnaby, instantaneous communications are maintained by microwave and fibre optics to allow remote control of all generating stations, transmission lines and switching stations in the entire provincial system. *B.C. Hydro*

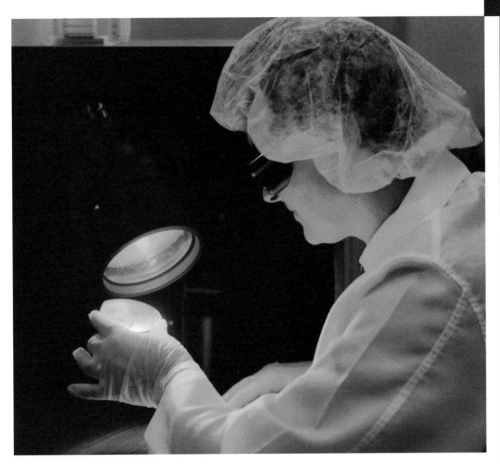

Wafers of gallium arsenide, a rare and costly metal, replace silicon wafers in advanced computers. Making these flaw-free wafers pushes science to its limits, and Cominco has introduced many innovations in their manufacture. Before sale, technicians examine wafers under ultraviolet light. *Jack La Rocque*

*W*e've had several years of experience with wireless terminals. Essentially, we have three applications: the terminals you see in City of Vancouver police cars, the terminals in taxis, and clipboard or tablet terminals.

In excess of 95 per cent of our annual revenues is from outside of Canada. It seems to me that our major opportunity is in learning to believe that we can do anything we set out to.

Barclay Isherwood
President, MDI Mobile Data
International Inc.

I don't think you're ever limited by where you live. But you have to keep communicating. With access to computers and a desire to do things, you aren't going to have many problems.

Working out on the leading edge is a little easier if you're concerned with hardware. To guess what's going to be leading edge in software in six months' time is really difficult.

I try to keep a positive attitude and do what makes me happy.

Don Mattrick
Software developer

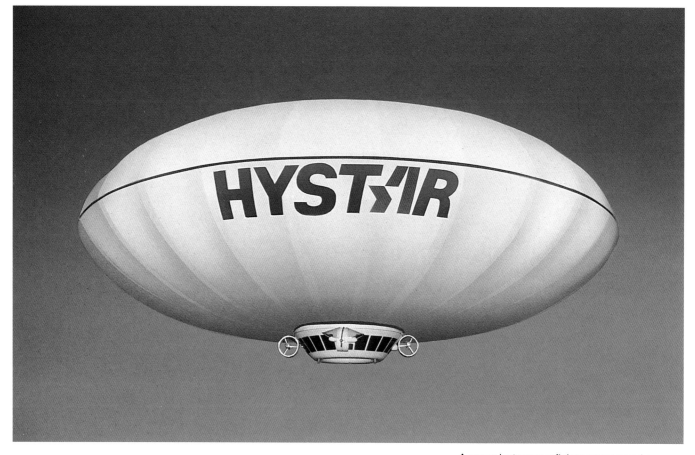

A cross between a flying saucer and a blimp, the Hystar aerodyne saucer was conceived by Vancouver's Hystar Aerospace Development Corporation. This newest flying machine, designed to replace helicopters in logging, may have applications in search-and-rescue, cargo transport, mining and agriculture.
Hystar Corporation

Parallam (parallel strand lumber) is a new wood material that is stronger than wood. Invented in British Columbia, Parallam promises to turn second-growth forests into first-rate lumber. Its unusual appearance is a result of the manufacturing process, in which long veneer strands are bonded together. The vertical wall mullions and horizontal cross-bracing in this structure are made of Parallam. *Peter Timmermans.*

We are going to have to come to grips with adjusting from a society that was comfortable with the tremendous demand for its resources to one that needs its wits to survive. We have a worldwide lead in supplying the needs of the forest industry and should be gearing up to manufacture specialized equipment — capitalize on our decades of experience at taking the trees out of the forests — and our newer understanding of how to put them back.

We need to unleash our imaginations.

Dr. Otto Forgacs
Senior Vice-President,
Research and Development,
MacMillan Bloedel Ltd.

There are more poor people than rich people in the world, and I just want to make a car for the poor people. When people think of car creators, they think about DeLorean and Bricklin. My car, the Rascal, is more like a sophisticated golf cart and uses off-the-shelf parts and can be manufactured anywhere in the world with a minimum amount of capital and technology.

Blythe Rogers
Industrial innovator

CELEBRATIONS

Hailed as an architectural and technological achievement, five magnificent teflon sails dominate the design of the new Vancouver trade and convention centre. The striking complex includes a cruise-ship facility and a large hotel. *Gary Fiegehen*

CELEBRATIONS

*C*elebration is whatever we do to honour, praise, remember and continue our association with each other and with our past.

Out of the pleasures and demands of hard work come many of the ways British Columbians celebrate. At town fairs, loggers hold ferocious competitions to see who is the quickest faller, climber or choker setter. Industrial first-aid teams compete to "save lives." Cowboys tour the rodeo circuit. Even waiters contend, gathering in Vancouver to race with a loaded tray held steady.

British Columbians are a sporting people. Sport is partly a celebration of human ability against the challenges of nature, and in few places does nature challenge more vigorously or provide surroundings with such great opportunities. Whether in deepest wilderness or as close as the peaks that overlook many cities and towns, skiers and climbers flock to the mountains. The ocean beckons, as do the many hundreds of lakes, and anything that will keep you afloat, from a million-dollar yacht to a rowboat, will do.

As it did a hundred years ago, exploration still motivates. In summer, the pickup-camper seems to be the most common vehicle on some B.C. highways. In winter, snowshoes, cross-country skis, ropes and karabiners get people to places no vehicle can reach.

Out of history, locale and purpose come other reasons for celebration in British Columbia. Countless communities, big and tiny, hold annual events with names like Timber Days and Sam Steele Days. Penticton's Peach Festival celebrates the Okanagan Valley's most luscious product. The Interior town of Barkerville celebrates the great gold rush of 1860. As earnest and proud as most towns are, though, a good sense of fun prevails.

The dramatic Museum of Anthropology at the University of British Columbia in Vancouver is home to the tall carved poles that once towered over native villages on the West Coast. *Simon Scott*

Facing page. As woodcarvers, the native people of British Columbia are justly renowned for their totem poles and other ceremonial and everyday objects. *Ken Straiton, Image Finders*

Previous page. Playland at Vancouver's Exhibition Park means a chance to be excited, delighted, turned upside-down, whirled around and around, and eat cotton candy all day long. *James O'Mara*

The land is also celebrated in the very proper gardens of Victoria, in the municipal, provincial and national parks, and in ways as small as the scenic stops along every highway. And Vancouver! Vancouver needs no excuse at all to celebrate; only a sunny day and half the town is promenading.

From the lovely Haida community centre on the beach near Queen Charlotte City to the grand Ismaili Jamatkhana of Burnaby, people celebrate their beliefs, their community and themselves. Homes and families, too, are important: from the high teas of Oak Bay to the pyroghies of Grand Forks, people celebrate their heritage through food and the rituals of preparing it.

Many of British Columbia's artists have attempted to portray the importance of the landscape in their lives and the lives of others. The paintings of Emily Carr powerfully depict the dark rain forests of B.C., but no work is more perfectly at home in B.C. than the carved totems and great canoes of the coastal native Indians. These ancient symbols of the land must have their place in contemporary celebration, and so it was appropriate that in the early 1970s B.C.'s greatest architect, Arthur Erickson, designed a magnificent monument to native culture, the Museum of Anthropology, incorporating native building styles into a modern structure.

British Columbia has this and more: folk art and avant-garde folks, logger-poets and computer musicians, cowboy crooners and Young Romantic painters, quilters and punkers, movie-makers and bagpipe blowers. They are all part of the lively and distinct ways that British Columbians celebrate their home and those who live in it.

Masks made by native people depicted an array of creatures — human, animal and mythic. Dancers wore masks to re-enact myths, spirit quests and other rituals. *Al Harvey*

Facing page. Once thought to be lost to the ravages of time and memory, native Indian art has been joyously and proudly reborn in recent decades. In Vancouver's Museum of Anthropology, Bill Reid's massive sculpture *Raven and the First Men* depicts the Haida legend of the beginning of man. Carved out of a huge block of 106 laminated yellow cedar beams, it took five people more than three years to complete. *Richard Krieger*

This idea of bringing Indian culture to a wider audience is very important. There was a time when native culture was something that was never acknowledged — never even mentioned.

Indian people are just now starting to come back to wanting to know about the old beliefs, the old teachings. There are more high-school Indian kids wanting to learn these things.

Now we sing our own songs and dance our own dances again.

George Clutesi
Actor, teacher, native
spokesman

We have some of the most fantastic visual artists in the world. There is only one Bill Reid. And Tony Onley wouldn't be painting the way he does if he weren't living on the West Coast.

And as for musical artists, Jon Kimura Parker is the very tip of the iceberg. Recently, an important judge of young musicians told me that she had never heard such an extraordinary collection of talent as here.

Leila Getz
Impresario

STIKINE: WILDERNESS RIVER

*H*igh up the side of an unnamed peak in Spatsizi Provincial Park in the northeast corner of the province, a glacier grudgingly recedes, releasing a silver stream to tumble down into Tuaton Lake. From here, British Columbia's Stikine River begins a tumultuous 650-kilometre-long passage through a land pushed up by volcanoes and slashed by glaciers to empty into the Pacific Ocean near Wrangell, Alaska.

The Stikine, divided into upper and lower rivers by its Grand Canyon, is the spawning ground of all five species of Pacific salmon. Bear, sheep, moose, deer, mountain goats and a number of smaller

1 High in the Cassiar Mountains, glacial runoff cuts a thin, silver stream across the Spatsizi Plateau and into Tuaton Lake. From here the Stikine flows until it reaches the Pacific Ocean.
2 Leaving only a trail of ripples to mark their passage, a moose and her calf make their unhurried way upriver.
3 Mount Edziza, whose last volcanic eruptions stained the mountainside with browns and reds, is part of the circum-Pacific "Ring of Fire." Dormant now for twelve hundred years, it still looks unwelcoming.

4

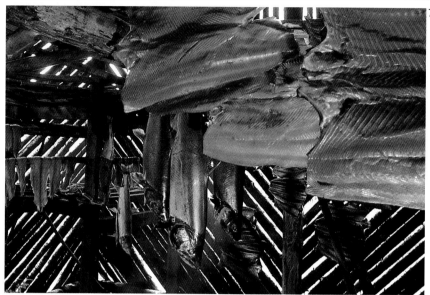

animals roam the adjoining forests and high plateaus. The only community along the river, Telegraph Creek, has a population of about two hundred, most of them Tahltan Indians, whose ancestral lands cover some of the Stikine watershed. A total of about one thousand people inhabit the entire 52 000 square kilometres of land that make up the watershed.

The land itself is more than just another area of wilderness. It is visible proof of how land can be shaped by the power of nature. The Stikine Plateau, near the source of the

4 With the morning mists still asleep in the valleys, a Tahltan guide rounds up the horses that have been grazing all night and brings them back to camp.

5 At Doug Blanchard's fishing camp on the lower Stikine, anglers have a chance at landing all five species of B.C. salmon that spawn in the river.

6 Tahltan guide Willie Williamson "glasses" for wildlife in the Mount Edziza area, the ancestral land of his people.

7 Salmon is the single largest contributor to the Tahltan economy. For centuries the native people have caught fish, and smoked and dried them for the winter.

9

river, was formed some six million years ago by the same volcanic forces that heaved up the mountains that surround it. Mount Edziza, in what is now Mount Edziza Park, was an active volcano as recently as twelve hundred years ago.

The magnificent Stikine is one of the last free-flowing rivers in North America. It and its major tributary, the Iskut River, and the countless smaller rivers and streams that swell them, have yet to be developed for industry or tourism.

8 Traditional native ways have not changed much for Fanny Woods who, at sixty-five, walks the 160 kilometres

from Telegraph Creek to her fishing camp and back each spring. In winter she traps, tans hides, makes moccasins and passes on her knowledge to young people like her granddaughter.

9 Tahltan guide Jim Bourguin, who takes tourists on trail and river expeditions, keeps his sled dogs in shape during the summer by getting them to pull a cart along the highway.

10 Some three hundred mountain goats live in the lower elevations of the Stikine's Grand Canyon. Clinging to the sheer canyon walls, they are oblivious to the water that churns past below.

11 Rich with sediment, the Stikine joins the Pacific Ocean. In the delta, shifting sandbars prevent navigation except at high tide.

Photographs by Gary Fiegehen

Seekers of solitude need only a backpack and desire. The land spreads its glories out as a feast for the eye and soul, often just hours from the noise and hurry of the city. *Pat Morrow, Image Finders*

Facing page. Whitewater rafters lean into their oars as they negotiate the rapids on the Chilcotin River. Once a sport reserved for daredevil thrillseekers, thousands of rafters now bounce and skim down B.C.'s wild rivers each year. *Robert Semeniuk*

B.C. is nature at her best, most generous and hospitable. We have valuable fish resources, attractive recreation areas, the most varied wildlife in North America, the finest timber, and huge reserves of coal and natural gas — all we have to do is manage it properly. It's our heritage and our heritage fund.

Dr. Peter Pearse
Resource economist

Etching the powder in perfectly symmetrical S-turns, heli-skiers carve a downhill design on a mountainside in the Cariboo Mountains. For the advanced and adventurous skiier, heli-skiing is an exhilarating change from standing in towlines.
Scott Rowed

Belts heavy with karabiners and the ropes that unite them with each other and against the mountain, climbers move up carefully. *David Falconer, Image Finders*

*T*ourism is the only industry in Canada that really is based on free trade. Tourists are free to cross borders, to spend their money wherever they want. To be successful we have to produce a vacation destination that is going to be as good as anywhere else in the world. We certainly have the natural beauty. Canada has it all.

But in order to build all the facilities that we need to compete on an international scale, tourist facilities require a reasonable chance for having year-round occupancy. The only chance we have of developing such vacation destinations is to combine the mountain/snow-and-ski experience with the equally attractive summer experience. This would include things like sightseeing attractions, outdoor recreation and activities like golf, watersports. If we do this, then we can really attract visitors.

After visiting the beaches of Yugoslavia and Italy, I appreciated as never before the natural beauty of our coast and the quality and cleanliness of our beaches. Nowhere else in the world has the gift that nature left been so respected by visitors.

Nancy Greene Raine
Proprietor, Nancy Greene's
Olympic Lodge

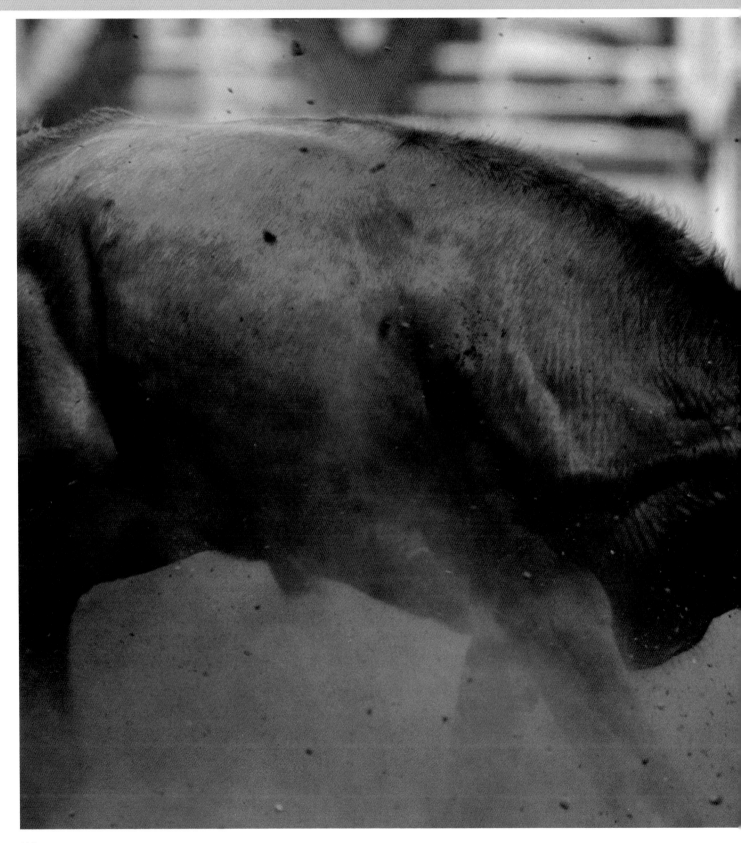

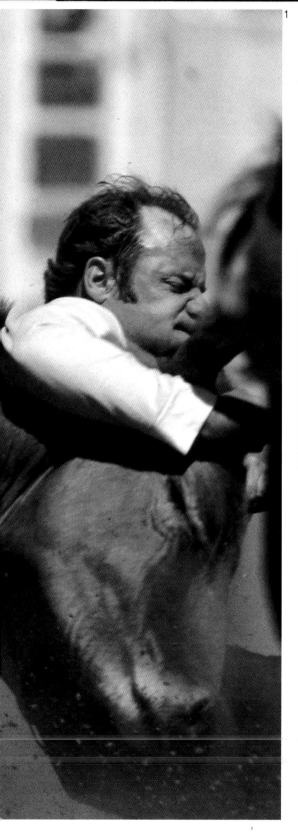

*A*t a point long before the adult forces of practicality play a part in decision-making, every child who straddles a stick horse vows to grow up to be a cowboy. A very few of them do. The rest go to rodeos.

Rodeos have been around as long as there have been ranches and cowboys. They began simply enough — after cowboys had spent long, dusty days on the range round-ing up cattle, breaking broncs, chasing steers and generally wearing themselves out doing these things for a living, they would get together and do them all over again for fun, competing against each other. They also added Brahma-bull riding, presumably because it was fun to try to spend eight seconds on the back of a tonne of lethal-horned animal whose ideas of fun differed quite violently from theirs.

1 After chasing the steer down, leaping from his horse onto him, and wrestling the beast to something approaching a halt, the cowboy is still faced with the challenge of making the beast lie down. Asking him nicely seldom helps.
2 Every so often, the animals score one.
3 Throw the campstove on the wagon, wait for the outriders to leap on their horses, circle the barrels, head for the track and hope the outriders catch up by the finish line — chuckwagon races are a sure crowd pleaser.
4 The funny face of a rodeo clown masks his serious job of protecting thrown or hurt cowboys in the arena.

119

5 There is just no holding back a dedicated urban cowboy!

6 A safe rule of thumb at a rodeo: the real cowboys are the ones who do not have rhinestones on their shirts.

7 The eight-second wait for the sound of the claxon can be rough when it takes place on the back of a tonne of bad-tempered Brahma bull.

8 For cowboys, the rodeo is a lot of waiting around for a ride that can end more quickly than planned.

Photographs by Robert Semeniuk (1–3, 5, 6); Brent Daniels (4); Patrick Hattenberger (7); Gunter Marx, Photo/Graphics (8)

Today in British Columbia the wild west may not be as wild as it used to be, but there is still a lot of cattle country, with ranches big and small. While ranches now are run with the help of a whole lot of modern technology the early ranchers did not have, nothing has yet replaced the cowboy on his horse for moving cattle.

Some fifty rodeos of varying sizes are held in British Columbia each year. Many of them are in the cattle-ranching areas of the Cariboo and Chilcotin. The largest and oldest of these is the Falklands Rodeo, first held sixty-five years ago and still going strong. Largest of all is the Cloverdale Rodeo, which attracts the top professional cowboys on the North American circuit and posts prize money of $130,000. The rodeo has come a long way from the early days in a dusty corral.

Yet the more the rodeo changes, the more it stays the same. No matter how simple or elaborate the trappings that surround the event, when the gates open and the bronc bucks out — then once again, just for a moment, everybody is a cowboy.

Originally from Russia, members of B.C.'s Doukhobor community pursue a life of simplicity and dignity. *Naomi Stevens*

Facing page, top. In front of an old house surrounded by Vancouver's towering office buildings, the "Birdhouse Man" has created an unexpected delight. *Doane Gregory*

Facing page, bottom. As individualistic as his brightly painted home, an elderly resident of Hedley surveys the world from his doorstep. *Lloyd Sutton*

*B*ritish Columbia — all of
Canada — is an experiment
in multiculturalism. There
are enormous stresses and
strains. By and large we are
successful in coping with
them. But we have to work to
guarantee that something
like the evacuation and
incarceration of Japanese
Canadians could never
happen again. I don't think it
will.

Dr. David Suzuki
Professor of Genetics, University of British Columbia,
and broadcaster

*B*ecause this is a frontier
province, we still have a
frontier spirit — we tend to
live for the moment. We're
also the last place you go in
Canada, so we have a lot of
newcomers. And we have the
idea that it doesn't matter
what happened before, we're
going to recreate the world —
remake the face of things.

Thomas R. Berger
Lawyer, jurist and writer

PENTICTON: HOME-TOWN WARMTH

1

1 Penticton grew up between the shores of Lake Okanagan and Skaha Lake. Originally named by the Indians *pen-tak-tin*, meaning "place to stay forever," it has attracted many who visit and later return to live.

2 When the Penticton Vees showed up in almost full force for their team reunion, the home-town heroes had been off the ice for about twenty years, but memories grew fresh when they lined up to match their old team photo.

3 *and* 4 Annie Adams came to Penticton from England at the age of sixteen. On her one hundredth birthday, her family gathered to share the celebration and her memories of a century.

When you grow up in a small town, the town stays with you. No matter how far you travel, "home" still means the warmth and familiarity and memories of communities like Penticton, and the good times and the old friends pull you back again and again.

In small communities, reunions take on a special significance. One year, Annie Adams, who came to Penticton in 1911, had her one hundredth birthday and her family gathered to celebrate. And at the same time there was a high-school reunion.

You can always find someone who will talk about the Penticton Vees (named for the three varieties of peaches grown nearby — Vedette, Valiant and Veteran), the home-town hockey team that won the Allan Cup in 1955. When, the next year, the Vees beat

the Russians 5-0 in the World Hockey Tournament, the town went crazy.

It is a treat to come home in the summertime, when the Peach Festival is on and the population is tripled by tourists. You can watch the parade that now gets two hundred entries and flock to the beach to join everyone else who is there cooling off under the hot Okanagan sky.

There is a saying that home is where they know all about you and like you anyway. Maybe that is why it is to the small towns all over the province that the city dwellers, every so often, come home.

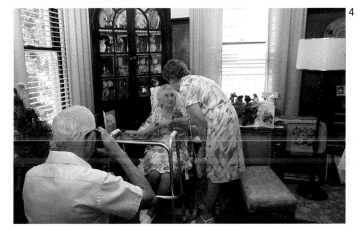

125

5

6

7

5, 6 and 7 With bands playing, floats
lined up and Mounties marching in
scarlet-coated splendour, the annual
Peachland Festival Parade is a sight.
And having the reunited Penticton Vees
riding along made this particular
parade very special.

8 No festival is complete without pretty
girls, and the Peach Festival has its
share of beauty queens to add sparkle
to the parade and the festival events.

*Photographs by Naomi Stevens (2–8) and
John Bartosik, Image Finders (1)*

Leisure earned is leisure enjoyed to the full. As a cruise ship makes its stately way along the coast, passengers have no larger decision than which sitting to take for lunch. *Rick Marotz, Photo/Graphics*

Facing page. Trim yachts crowd Victoria harbour, as they have since 1930, on the eve of the annual Swiftsure Race. The 210-kilometre race takes the boats out into Juan de Fuca Strait to Swiftsure Bank and back again. *P. Andras Dancs, North Light Images*

The tourist industry is going to be the number one industry in this province. It's just a question of what year it's going to take the lead. We have a big, big job to do, in the tourist industry. We have to be committed to excellence.

Jim Pattison
Chairman of the Board,
Expo 86

Changes in our harbour city of Nanaimo have been much the same as the changes in Vancouver Island in general. For instance, many people move here in search of a high quality of life. It's hard to beat our recreational opportunities — our mountains, oceans, hunting, fishing, skiing. And if you're raising children, this is a good place to do it. There's also a great opportunity to involve oneself and get to know people here.

As far as tourism is concerned, I think we just haven't beaten the drum loudly enough about how fantastic this province really is. We need to work on a plan that will broadcast our pride in our own communities. We need to show tourists those things about our towns that the local citizens appreciate for twelve months a year.

Graeme Roberts
Mayor of Nanaimo

*F*rom March to October we run ten-day programs where we take the kids out and let them get the feel of a big sailing ship. Those kids come from all over. Once they're on board they realize quickly that there are rules to follow in order to sail the ship. That isn't always something they take to too kindly at first. But by the fourth or fifth day things start making sense. And real teamwork comes about through this realiza-tion — that there is a purpose for the order of things. Discipline is taught this way. We sail with a thousand kids a year and virtually without exception they want to come back. They cannot remain unchanged by the experience.

What we'd like to do eventually is set up a full year program and then make a voyage along the Pacific Rim.

Martyn Clark
President, Sail and Life
Training Society

Heeling heavily as the sails strain to take on more wind, yachts own English Bay on a blowy afternoon. Dozens of yacht clubs and marinas dot the province's coastline to cater to those who respond to the call of the sea. *Carolyn Angus, Photo/Graphics*

Facing page. Spinnakers unfurled to trap the slightest wind, a Sunday afternoon fleet of pleasure boats heads for home past the lighthouse at Point Atkinson off West Vancouver. *Al Harvey*

The legend of John Peel lives on in British Columbia as scarlet-jacketed members of the Richmond Hunt obey the call to hounds in the vanishing morning mists. *James O'Mara*

Facing page. While courts around the province are usually full of eager players dawn to dusk and beyond, tennis in British Columbia does bow to one opponent: the weather. *Jacques André*

Next page. At the end of his run-up, a bowler delivers his leather cricket ball at speeds of more than 145 kilometres an hour. *Chuck O'Rear, Image Finders*

*F*or me, everything always related to rhythmics. I've tried lots of other things but I just keep coming back. It works best for me. I think I'll always be involved in sport. Sometimes there are interesting tie-ins, though. Recently, I did a couple of routines on the stage of Roy Thompson Hall in Toronto for a special Gala Tribute to Roland Michener. It was wonderful, and the response from the audience was overwhelming. Afterwards, somebody from the National Ballet came up and asked if I'd like to dance with them. I think that would be really neat.

Since B.C. athletes did so well in the last Olympics, things have progressed fairly well. With funding and development plans and so on. And you know, that's really always the problem. We need support to win the gold, but so much of the support only comes after. But then I guess it's hard for the government to know who to support without some kind of track record. How do you decide among the hundreds of kids who say they're after the gold?

Lori Fung
Olympic gold medallist (1984),
rhythmic gymnast

"Since my accident two major dreams inspired me. One is to help those people with spinal injuries and the other is to wheel around the world. Through the Man in Motion World Tour, I know I can realize both dreams." B.C. athlete Rick Hansen. *Tim Pelling*

Facing page. Concerned citizens of all ages and walks of life make speeches, wave banners and present statements each spring at Vancouver's annual peace march, which has the largest turnout in Canada. *Marin Petkov, Photo/Graphics*

*I*n the early days we were a very provincial place: mentally as well as culturally isolated. Now, we are growing more interested in national and international affairs. We're still a country that is very aware of its regions, but I think that we are finally coming to have more a national conscience. We seem to be gradually getting our affairs in order.

We have come to realize that there are great concerns in the world that far outstrip in importance the immediate affairs of British Columbia. We are now interested in things that happen outside our own borders. This is very good.

Bruce Hutchison,
Writer, political commentator

137

ART FOUNDRY: IDEAS IN BRONZE

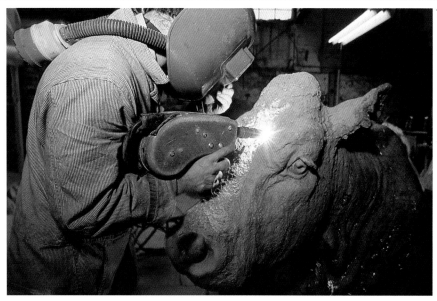

1

1 Looking more bovine at every step of the process, each cow is welded together with invisible seams.
2 Casting and finishing Joe Fafard's herd of cows was an eleven-month job for the foundry. Molten bronze is poured into the mold, where it will melt the packing and take on its intended shape.
3 Each of the bronze cows weighs in at 500 kilograms, so moving them around the foundry is a big job.
4 The bronze herd in its final grazing ground amid skyscrapers in downtown Toronto.

Photographs by Tim Pelling

*T*he casting of bronze into sculpture: in the painstaking journey from a creation in the mind of an artist to a finished piece that will last for centuries, the foundry is the link that translates concept into reality.

Perhaps because he is a sculptor himself, Jack Harman's art foundry in Vancouver is one of the most highly respected in Canada for the exceptional quality of its work.

Many sculptors have their works cast into metal at the Harman Foundry, knowing that their works will receive the respect of an artist for the art form. Joe Fafard's *The Pasture*, a herd of seven bronze cows that graze forever in front of the Toronto-Dominion Centre in Toronto, enjoyed the fine touch of skilled workers at this specialized foundry.

Though blind Justice weighs her judgement still according to tradition, Arthur Erickson's courthouse on Robson Square in the heart of Vancouver is breathtakingly modern. The concrete, glass and steel structure, acclaimed as an architectural coup, is a distinctive new landmark. *Gary Fiegehen*

Facing page. Built in 1898, the Legislative Buildings in Victoria were designed by Francis Rattenbury, also the architect of the Empress Hotel and the old courthouse (now art gallery) in Vancouver. Much of the stone came from B.C. quarries: granite foundations from Nelson Island, andesite facade from Haddington and slate roof from Jervis Inlet. *Bruce Rutherford*

I tend to take a structural approach to landscape and a landscape approach to architecture. Perhaps this tendency grew out of my love for the evocative landscape of British Columbia, where I was deeply initiated into the world of nature. I could never conceive of a building apart from its setting.

Arthur Erickson
Architect

*I*f I were to characterize the art scene in B.C., I'd say that what we have is a three-tiered system. We have some very fine, established artists whose work is consistently excellent — Gordon Smith, Jack Shadbolt, Toni Onley and E. J. Hughes. In the middle ground we have the brighter, fresher artists such as Gathie Falk. Then we have the up-and-comers — mostly they're young, in many cases only a few years out of art school. And of course we mustn't forget Northwest Coast native art. I mean in terms of what is happening now and not just important past work. There is a revitalization of native art taking place, with Bill Reid, Robert Davidson, Norman Tate and others.

Ron Longstaffe
Collector, patron of the arts,
businessman

141

Art in British Columbia is often influenced by the landscape, but also by more personal statements like those of painter, sculptor and performance artist Gathie Falk. *Kate Williams*

Facing page, top and bottom. Located where the streets of Vancouver turn a cultural corner into the different world that is Chinatown, Dr. Sun Yat-Sen Park is a one-hectare sanctuary. With the care of a master craftsman, a lacquerer (bottom) works on one of the structures in the Park. This Ming Dynasty–style garden is the only classical Chinese garden outside China, and a tranquil addition to this, North America's second-largest Chinese community. *Albert Chin*

In the current world economic crisis, Canada stands at a crossroads, with British Columbia having a unique role to play for Canada.

With the Asia Pacific region's dynamic emergence as a centre of world economic and cultural vitality, we have within our grasp a whole new dimension of opportunity — but only if we make a concerted effort to shape a role for ourselves as a member of the Pacific community.

This situation is graphically described by the Chinese symbol for "crisis," which consists of two components: the top character signifies "danger"; the bottom character signifies "opportunity." Which one it will be for Canada depends on our resolve and our actions in a changing world. It especially depends on the resolve and the actions of British Columbia, which is in the forefront of this unique opportunity.

John Bruk
Chairman and Director, Asia
Pacific Foundation of Canada

143

Young Korean Canadian girls at Vancouver's annual Asia Pacific festival, which features exciting entertainers from Pacific Rim countries and hundreds of local performers in a week of song, dance and food. *Randy Martin*

Having climbed to the top of the slide, a
boy at a Parksville playground pauses to
give his situation some serious thought.
Gordon Lafleur

We are facing an economic challenge as we learn that our economy can't be entirely resource-oriented. This is a challenge for the next generation. And of course the other challenge is for us to see that our young people get a very, very good education. This should be our priority.

We need to take a cue from the Japanese — who have come so far since the war, and all in a country that has almost no natural resources except brain power. They understand the benefits of education.

If we're not careful, we'll have another brain drain — just like we had in the Thirties.

Once we recognize that our principal resource in the future is going to be well-trained young people, we'll be in a much better situation to face the future.

The Hon. N. T. Nemetz
Chief Justice of British
Columbia

GRANVILLE ISLAND: CITY HEART

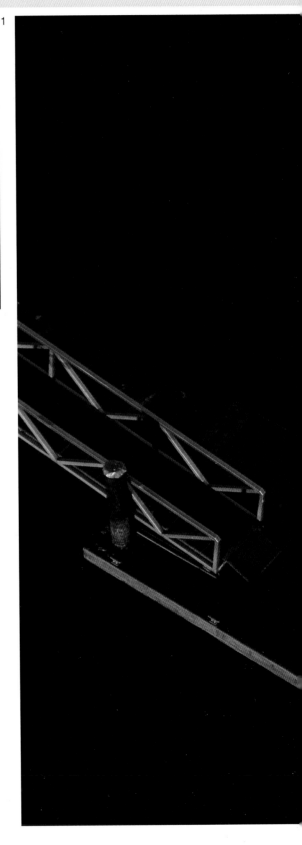

*I*t glows with neon, it teems with excitement; it is wild, wonderful, more fun than a day at the circus, and it grew out of a 14-hectare mud pie in Vancouver's False Creek. It is Granville Island and is like no other place in the province.

Granville Island was not even an island until 1913. It was tidal flats when the tide was out and under a couple of metres of water when the tide was in. Seven hundred and forty thousand cubic metres of fill later,

1 Many industries have left the island, but the cement plant owned by Ocean Construction is a vital part of the place's commercial/industrial mix.
2 On sunny days, and even rainy ones, city dwellers flock to the island to stroll, shop and meet friends.
3 The Emily Carr College of Art was one of the first institutions to claim a spot when redevelopment was announced. Its corrugated iron sides and bright signage fit right in with the island's industrial heritage and decor.
4 Looking for all the world like a favourite bathtub toy that grew, the Aquabus ferry shuttles passengers between Granville Island and downtown Vancouver.

2

3

4

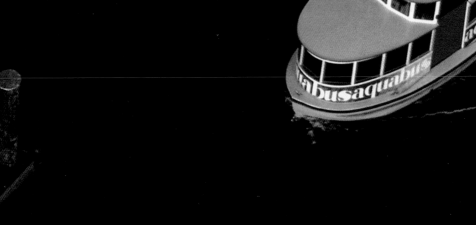

147

6 it was named Mud Island, was permanently above water and home to about forty industrial businesses. By the end of the 1930s, it really was not an island any more either; another two hectares of fill and it was connected to the shore and renamed Granville Island.

Not one of Vancouver's most scenic areas, it continued to be home to industry until 1972. At that point the federal government, under some pressure from local representatives, took a deep breath and opted for the fairly radical urban renewal scheme that created Granville Island. Industry would, for the most part, be relocated. In its stead, a bright busy, exciting and joyful place for people would be created. It was a concept that had been tried with varying degrees of success in other cities and was thought to be a wild notion for the somewhat staid heart of downtown Vancouver. Amid more than a

7 little scepticism, most of the industry left (leaving behind, however, the shells of their buildings), a seawall was built and renovations of the warehouses were begun.

The Granville Island Public Market was the first big development in the new plan, and the one that planners felt would make or break the scheme. Four old warehouses were joined together, leaving lots of room along the water for good weather strolling and eating; and by July 1979, the huge building was filled with twenty-six stalls, more fresh fruit, produce, meat and fish than Vancouver had seen in one place before, and the fervent hopes of the federal government that it would take off. They need not have worried: Granville Island was an instant hit.

Other renovated industrial buildings now house restaurants, shops, food outlets, offices, a brewery, theatres, a waterside hotel (with room service to the boats

8

docked in its marina), the Emily Carr College of Art and Design, a permanent houseboat community, specialty stores, and even a few of the original industries, the largest of which is Ocean Construction's giant cement plant.

This unlikely potpourri co-exists colourfully and conveniently right in the heart of the city, drawing thousands of residents and visitors daily. While the buildings have been painted and renovated, the industrial character has to some extent been preserved. Small boats sail between the island and the north shore of False Creek, ferrying people who do not want to drive or bus to the island. Pleasurecraft from luxury yachts to small kayaks tie up along the seawall and in the marinas. The Public Market, now expanded to forty stalls, offers everything from stuffed quail to fresh bread to fish right off the boat, and mounds of the Lower Mainland's finest fruits and vegetables.

5 Some people think it is more fun to drink their fruit than to eat it, and merchants at the Public Market have elevated the simple glass of juice to a gourmet concoction.

6 Countless loaves of French bread, enough to satisfy the appetites of an army of shoppers, is rolled out ready for the ovens in one of the island's bakeries.

7 If it has fins or a shell and lives in the waters of the Strait of Georgia, it will undoubtedly be on sale at the Public Market.

8 One Granville Island fruitseller has turned advertising into an appealing, homey art.

9 Other stores may be closer to home, but the atmosphere of the Public Market draws people from all over the Lower Mainland. Where else can you pick up turkey sausage or suckling pig, eat sushi or tortillas for lunch, and watch the boats on the water — all in the same place?

9

While Granville Island is one of the city's most popular places to shop, it is also very much what it was intended to be in the beginning — a "people place."

10 Neon flashes along the underside of Granville Bridge at the entrance to Granville Island. Until 1913, this entire area was under water at high tide.

11 The cast members of *Ain't Misbehavin'* are among the top performers who appear at the Arts Club Revue Theatre — and the other theatres on Granville Island.

12 One of the many popular restaurants on the island, this spot combines an elegant seafood restaurant with a bistro, a pub and a wide deck for good-weather dining and socializing.

13 Vancouver's marine industry has naturally gravitated to Granville Island. Serious sailors can negotiate for yachts costing hundreds of thousands of dollars while those who just want to look like sailors can shop nearby for the proper clothes.

Photographs by Robert Semeniuk (1–2, 4–13) and Ross Stojko, Image Finders (3)

THE B.C. PAVILION STORY

*I*n 1986, just a hundred years after the great railway united a sprawling land into the world's second-largest nation, Canada's westernmost province invited the world to a celebration. From its fortunate geographical location halfway between Asia and Europe, British Columbia, a seasoned world trader, was accustomed to venturing forth. Now, the province was opening its doors and inviting the world to share a pivotal time in its history, moving from a resource-based economy to a diversified one involving high technology and manufacturing.

The celebration took the form of a World Exposition. Its theme, transportation and communications, was appropriate both to a rapidly shrinking globe and to a province where these technologies were fundamental to survival and development.

Vancouver, Canada's third-largest and most beautiful city, supplied a perfect fair site on the water with a backdrop of mountains. And at centre stage in the 70-hectare assembly of forty-five nations was the British Columbia Pavilion, ready to welcome the world.

Designing the B.C. Pavilion was a challenge. The job was this: to fit a province

1 Situated in the heart of Vancouver, the B.C. Pavilion
buildings will be remodelled
after the fair and will remain
as a permanent legacy of
EXPO 86 for the future benefit
of British Columbians.
2 A geometry of steel frames a
construction worker as he
completes the glass canopy
high above the Plaza of
Nations.
3 Mud, trucks and steel
characterize the early
construction stages of the
pavilion complex on
Vancouver's False Creek.

4 Lattices of steel covered by glass bridge the Plaza of Nations. Under this transparent roof, thousands of people can gather for outdoor events and ceremonies.

5 A traditional-style building contrasts charmingly with contemporary Expo images: the aquamarine glass of the B.C. Pavilion and the Expo Centre's shining geodesic dome.

6 The B.C. Pavilion's distinctive entry gates celebrate the colour and exuberance of the province's waving flag symbol.

7 Under construction, the exhibit highlights of the B.C. Pavilion — the Trees of Discovery — rise 30 metres and incorporate an innovative exterior design with unique interior multimedia rides.

4 — nearly a million square kilometres and nearly three million people — into 4.5 hectares of Vancouver waterfront; to use steel and glass, performance and whimsy, to celebrate the people, magnificence and prospects of British Columbia. And more: the buildings and exhibits would have to embody the great pride we felt both in our province and as host of a world fair, in a way that would satisfy the most critical audience of all — the people of British Columbia. The pavilion would be not only an entry to the fair but a welcome to visitors to the province and a reminder of home to British Columbians. And above all, the pavilion had to retain the feeling of entertainment and excitement of a fair.

Adding to the challenge was the desire for a structure that would become a permanent legacy for the people of British Columbia rather than one designed simply to display exhibitry during the fair. But challenges are what British Columbia is all about — and with the pavilion, as with the province throughout its history, the answer was innovation.

What rose on the long, narrow, curving Expo site was not just one building, but a complex: three structures and a huge, glass-roofed plaza — the Plaza of Nations — forming a common ground. On the plaza, up to 10 000 people could enjoy the fair's major events and ceremonies. The most striking of the three pavilion buildings is a high, vaulted geometry of steel ribbing and glass that juts into the waters of False Creek like a glittering chunk of aquamarine crystal.

Exhibitry itself was another challenge: it had to celebrate and entertain, as well as educate and market. In the long process of creating the presentations, researchers were excited to find they were putting together the definitive statement of who, what and

why we are. But how to present it all and share those insights? There was no one solution, but a combination of many.

In the first pavilion building, Discovery B.C., innovative designers created many intimate worlds within the soaring, transparent structure. Some of these worlds were contained in the Trees of Discovery, four smooth, space-age "totems" that dramatically rose to the top of the building. Inside the trees, visitors went on multimedia voyages beneath the sea, as well as to look at today's high-tech world and even beyond into tomorrow.

A different kind of voyage awaited audience's in Discovery B.C.'s Showscan Theatre, where designers took advantage of a dazzling, new high-resolution film technology to sweep viewers along on an adventure through the province's spectacular landscape. For a closer look, another presentation beckoned visitors to stroll through re-creations of the province's varied regions and character.

Pavilion planners turned the waterfront location into a wonderful asset by using real boats to show the province's long-standing love affair with the sea. Here, visitors could get close up views of innovative submersibles designed and built in B.C., heritage vessels and a variety of working boats.

The second pavilion building, Challenge B.C., had the problem of presenting the story of industry in the province in an entertaining way. In some ways this was the toughest assignment, but again designers came up with a solution: an appealing mix of live performance, multimedia special effects — and humour. These components formed the pre-show that introduced a second film, which reached out to viewers, making the fabric of life in B.C. tangible by taking them along on a real day with real

people who live and work in this province.

Meanwhile, as the buildings and displays took shape, the whole province was becoming involved. In collaboration with the Ministry of Education, the pavilion developed a special social studies course for schools across British Columbia. A mobile pavilion presentation went out on the road to share the excitement of the coming fair with British Columbians. The pavilion also consulted and involved a variety of community groups and industries across the province in the development of exhibitry to reflect their ideas and priorities. More than ninety local committees thought up ways to enhance the attractions of their home towns for visitors who would carry on travelling in B.C. after attending the fair. And, as the pavilion flowed out to the province, the province was also flowing in to the pavilion. For the pavilion's regional weeks programme, communities across British Columbia sent entertainers, festivals and special foods to help welcome visitors.

For British Columbians, the pavilion offered an opportunity to celebrate the province's accomplishments, people and culture, a chance to become better acquainted with their own home and neighbours. For others, who may have never set foot in B.C. before, the pavilion was a basic introduction to the province, as well as an invitation to explore, to return, even to invest. If the pavilion had wanted only to impress people with the beauty of the province, the task would have been simple. But this was a once-in-a-lifetime opportunity for the province to reveal itself

on the world stage, and the B.C. Pavilion succeeded admirably in presenting our history, distinctive regions, tourist information, resource management and high technology with humour and verve.

Discovery and challenge have always been a part of the history of British Columbia from the time of the early explorers to present-day research into the possibilities of the unknown. Discovery and challenge were also key themes in the B.C. Pavilion and resulted in not only telling the world about British Columbia but finding out much about ourselves. And, during that eventful year when we reached out to the world from the B.C. Pavilion, we delighted in sharing this special time of our lives.

8 Thousands of balloons signal the completion of another stage of pavilion construction while bare flagpoles await the colours of fifty-two participating nations, provinces, territories and states.

9 Virtually every community and segment of society in the province became involved in the Expo experience. In readiness to Host the World, Premier William R. Bennett officially dedicates the B.C. Pavilion Complex to the people of British Columbia.

10 Even before EXPO 86 opened, the Plaza of Nations delighted crowds of visitors who came to see "Christmas on the Plaza" in December 1985. This twinkling magic was the forerunner of the fair's vibrant night life.

Photographs by Peter Timmermans (1-8, 10) and Creative House (9)

ABOUT THE PHOTOGRAPHERS

Derek and Jane Abson emigrated from England in 1980. They have lived in South Africa, where they won awards for wildlife photography. Now residing in Port Coquitlam, they are avid travellers and outdoor photographers.

Jacques André was born in Victoria; in 1984 he graduated from the Emily Carr College of Art and Design with honours in photography. He is freelancing in Vancouver, where he specializes in architectural and editorial photography.

Carolyn Angus, a native Montrealer, was "captivated by the boldness of B.C." and moved west permanently in 1979. She is a world traveller, is trilingual, studied executive portraiture in New York City and loves sailing photography.

Mark Atherton studied photography in the United States and lives in Vancouver. He specializes in underwater and architectural subjects, as well as being Technical Manager at Can-Dive, where he is in charge of television, acoustics and photography.

John Bartosik was born in Oshawa, Ontario, and trained in motion pictures and photography at Ryerson Polytechnic. He specializes in tourism-related images, and he has also published a book of his photographs, *Sea to Sky Country.*

Dolores Baswick left Hamilton, Ontario, in 1980 and moved to Vancouver, where she maintains a studio, works as a professional commercial photographer and enjoys sailing.

Peter Bennett is involved full-time in editorial, audiovisual, travel, corporate and publishing assignments and also teaches travel photography. His photographs and travel writing have appeared in Canadian, British and African publications.

Randy Bradley, an artist and photographer for fifteen years, has taught photography at the Banff Centre School of Fine Arts and the Emily Carr College of Art and Design. His work is in several collections, including that of the National Gallery of Canada.

Thomas Bruckbauer left West Germany in 1982. He has a studio in Chilliwack and is a professional editorial photographer as well as a teacher of photography at Fraser College.

Albert Chin left Hong Kong in 1967 and studied fine arts at the University of British Columbia. He is a commercial photographer in Vancouver and specializes in stock photography and annual reports; his clients have included Tourism B.C. and Expo 86.

P. Andras Dancs is an award-winning photographer. His work is in the permanent collection of the National Archives of Canada. In 1985 the Professional Photographers of Canada granted him two awards.

Brent Daniels has lived most of his life in Vancouver. He studied photography at Langara College and is now a full-time commercial photographer who also does some editorial work. A number of his images appear on internationally distributed art posters.

David Falconer, Vancouver-born, has spent much of his life as a photojournalist and was for twenty-five years the Portland *Oregonian's* staff photographer. He resides in Portland where, when he is not mountain climbing, he is a free-lance editorial photographer.

Dr. R. A. Farquhar and his camera have travelled extensively in many parts of the world. He lives with his family in Kelowna.

Gary Fiegehen studied photographic arts at Ryerson Polytechnic in Toronto. In 1973 he moved to Vancouver and free-lanced as a strictly commercial photographer. The Stikine River watershed is a close personal interest, and a book of the photographic results is in progress.

Ed Gifford came to Canada in 1974 after studying fine arts and English in New Mexico. He specializes in advertising and corporate communications, and is also devoted to art education. He co-founded CREO[3], a nonprofit art gallery and school.

Doane Gregory is a Vancouver-based free-lance photojournalist and editorial photographer for a variety of magazines. He and his camera have travelled extensively throughout the South Pacific and Asia.

Greg Hall was born in Vancouver and is a registered professional engineer. A professional photographer for over two years, he specializes in aerial photography.

Al Harvey is a native of Vancouver and has, since 1978, been photographing mostly for corporate, institutional and government multi-image presentations. As well, he maintains an extensive collection of stock photography.

Patrick Hattenberger came to Vancouver from France and started his studio in 1981. He is a full-time advertising, editorial and fashion photographer, whose work has won several international Nikon photography awards.

Image West Photography consists of co-partners Rick Blacklaws and Vance Hanna. Rick has an M.A. in archaeology and has been a professional photographer for five years. Vance has worked as a professional photographer for the past decade and has won several Professional Photographers of Canada awards.

Colin Jewall was born in Winnipeg. Trained in the engineering field, he has been a full-time photographer for five years, specializing in architectural, aerial and commercial subjects.

Richard Krieger came from the San Francisco Bay area and lives in Victoria, where he is a construction contractor, professional bee-keeper and part-time photographer. His work has appeared in many magazines, and books such as *Islands at the Edge.*

Gordon Lafleur studied photography in Alberta and has worked as a commercial photographer since 1971. In 1973 he came to British Columbia and now operates a photo studio in Parksville.

Jack La Rocque lives in Fruitvale (near Trail) and has worked as an industrial photographer for Cominco for thirty-seven years. His work formed part of an exhibit at the Museum of Man in Ottawa.

Lou Lehmann came to Vancouver from Germany in 1958. A sport diver, he has been an underwater photographer since 1968 and specializes in marine biology.

Dale Leniuk has been active as both a photographer and a multimedia producer since 1974. His specialty is corporate-industrial media programs covering a variety of companies and locations in North America and abroad.

Don McRae is a lifelong Vancouver Island resident. Combining his hobbies of flying and photography, he set up a free-lance aerial photography company, providing shots for corporate clients. He no longer photographs, but still flies.

Rick Marotz, a self-taught photographer, came to Vancouver from Germany thirty years ago. He specializes in scenic and people photographs, but does some architectural work. He had a one-man show at the Burnaby Art Gallery in 1968 and won the gold medal at the 1982 B.C. International Exhibition.

Randy Martin describes himself as a street photographer. He has taught English in the Far East and now teaches it in Vancouver. Besides being a part-time, free-lance photographer, he is an avid squash player.

Gunter Marx, who came to Canada from West Germany in 1963, has travelled and hiked extensively throughout British Columbia. His photographs of the province have appeared in magazines and books and have won awards in provincial, national and international exhibitions.

Pat Morrow, an adventure photographer and photojournalist, documents noncompetitive recreations such as mountain climbing and hot-air ballooning. He was a member of the Canadian Everest Expedition in 1982. His book *Quest for the Seventh Mountain* looks at the world from a climber's perspective.

Michelle Normoyle, born in Ottawa, moved to Vancouver in 1973 and has been photographing construction sites since 1982. She graduated from the Emily Carr College of Art and Design in 1984, and her work has been in several group shows across Canada, as well as a one-woman show at the Or Gallery.

James O'Mara has lived in Vancouver for fifteen years. As a graphic designer he has created about fifty album covers; as a filmmaker he has produced and directed documentaries, and as a photographer he has shot advertising stills. He is working with Arthur Erickson on a film on indigenous architecture.

Chuck O'Rear resides in California's Napa Valley. As a free-lance photographer, he has shot at least thirteen major stories for *National Geographic* magazine and recently provided technology photographs for the book *Silicon Valley: Hi-Tech Window to the Future.*

Tim Pelling, a Vancouver photographer and sculptor, graduated from the Emily Carr College of Art and Design. He is working as a free-lance photographer, doing mainly editorial and industrial work. A major recent project of his has been to document Rick Hansen's Man in Motion world tour.

Marin Petkov, who came to Vancouver from Czechoslovakia in 1975, is a "self-assigned" part-time photographer. He specializes in architectural and scenic photography and enjoys shooting the Vancouver skyline. He has exhibited at several shows in Vancouver.

Martin Roland grew up in Edmonton, graduated in political science, then moved to Vancouver and became addicted to photography. He now does a mix of photographic work including commercial, editorial and portrait, as well as personal work, which he is developing into slide/tape productions.

Scott Rowed lives in Banff and works as a heli-skiing guide. A professional photographer for eight years, he specializes in outdoor, nature, travel and sports. His work appears in magazines, including *National Geographic.*

Bruce Rutherford, originally from Owen Sound, Ontario, has lived in Victoria for the past eight years. He was a news photographer but now works free lance.

Simon Scott came to Vancouver from England in 1966. First on his own and then with Arthur Erickson Architects, he specialized in architectural photography and presentations. He worked in Rome with the late Roloff Beny on his book *In Italy* and photographed for and designed *The Architecture of Arthur Erickson.*

Robert Semeniuk was born in Alberta and graduated from York University with a master's degree in environmental studies. Based in Vancouver, he travels widely on writing and photography assignments for major corporations and magazines. His work is published internationally through Black Star in New York City.

Naomi Stevens, since graduating from the Brooks Institute, has worked in film and video and currently free-lances in Vancouver, where she specializes in stills work for corporate and audiovisual and editorial clients.

Ross Stojko's images frequently appear on cards and art prints. He is self-taught and now lives and photographs in Terrace Bay, Ontario. In 1985 he received an Art Directors Award for travel photography.

Ken Straiton is a full-time photographer who currently lives and works in Tokyo. He has shown his work at the Emily Carr College of Art and Design in Vancouver. Also, he was a member of the Canadian Everest Expedition in 1982.

Lloyd Sutton left Winnipeg for Vancouver in 1981 and worked for *Beautiful B.C.* magazine. Now a full-time free lance, he is an industrial and location specialist. Some of his images were included in a show at the EPCOT Center in 1985.

Peter Timmermans came to Vancouver from West Germany in 1980. An architect by trade, he is now a full-time stock photographer specializing in commercial and architectural subjects. His extensive library of Vancouver and Expo photographs has appeared in magazines nationwide.

Jürgen Vogt, a self-taught photojournalist, left Berlin for Canada shortly after the war. His first photographs appeared in *Time* in 1970, and since then he has covered events in Poland, Italy, the U.S. and Canada for many publications. He also does landscape and travel photography.

Stirling Ward is a commercial-illustrative photographer whose studio is in Vancouver. He has many regional, national and international awards to his credit, including New York CLIO finalist, and is the appointed photographer for Expo 86.

Kate Williams, a resident of Victoria, was born in Chatham, Ontario, and studied at Conestoga College. She has been a free-lance photographer since 1973, and her work appears often in national publications.

Doug Wilson, a professional photographer for twenty-six years, specializes in people, agriculture and industry. His work has appeared in over a hundred magazines, including *Time, Life* and *Newsweek.*

PUBLICATION STAFF

Writers: Scott Mowbray
　　　　Marnie Huckvale
Editor: Saeko Usukawa
Art Director: Barbara Hodgson
Co-ordinator: Michael Scott
Photo Researcher: Kate Poole
Editorial Researcher: Laura Coles

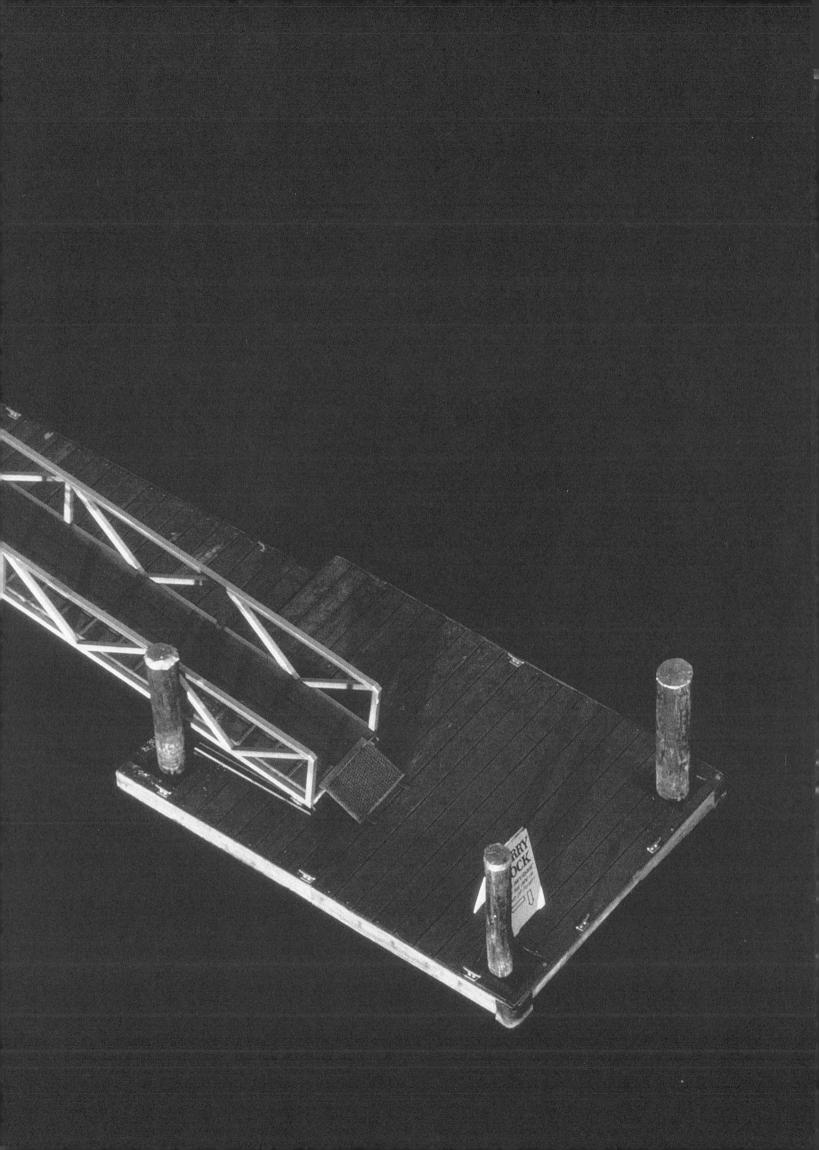